SOUTH WALES
BRANCH LINES

SOUTH WALES BRANCH LINES

H. MORGAN

LONDON

IAN ALLAN LTD

The Alexandra (Newport & South Wales) Docks & Railway

The ADR was incorporated by an Act of Parliament dated 6 July 1865, as the Alexandra (Newport) Dock Company. Because of delays — originally caused by the difficulty of raising capital during the general uncertainty after the financial crisis of 1866 — the North Dock was not opened till 10 April 1875. The company had short connecting lines to the GWR and the Monmouthshire Railway & Canal Co; and in 1882 it changed its title to the later form — the Alexandra (Newport & South Wales) Docks & Railway. In 1884 it absorbed the Newport Dock Co, which had been incorporated in 1835 to build the Town Dock. This had opened in 1842 and was further extended in 1858.

In 1878 the Pontypridd, Caerphilly & Newport Railway (PC&NR) was promoted so that coal from the Aberdare and Rhondda Valleys could be shipped through Newport Docks. On 8 August 1878 Parliament granted an Act to a truncated form of this proposal. It was to run between a junction with the Taff Vale Railway (TVR) at Pontypridd and a junction with the Rhymney Railway at Caerphilly, by means of running powers over the Brecon and Merthyr Railway's (B&MR) Caerphilly branch to Bassaleg, from where it was hoped that the B&MR's running powers over the former Monmouthshire Railway & Canal Co would be sufficient to gain access to the ADR at West Mendalgyf Junction.

The TVR contracted to work the PC&NR coal trains to the Alexandra Docks, in the hope that this would lead to the PC&NR becoming part of its growing system. The first train of coal left Pontypridd on 7 July 1884 calling at Caerphilly to take on a B&MR pilot engine. However on arrival at Bassaleg the GWR declined to allow the PC&NR train to pass over the junction. After a couple of weeks of negotiations the GWR gave way and the PC&NR coal trains began to run to the Alexandra Docks in earnest from 25 July 1884.

The ADR had in 1883 obtained an Act authorising the construction of its own double line between Bassaleg and West Mendalgyf Junc-

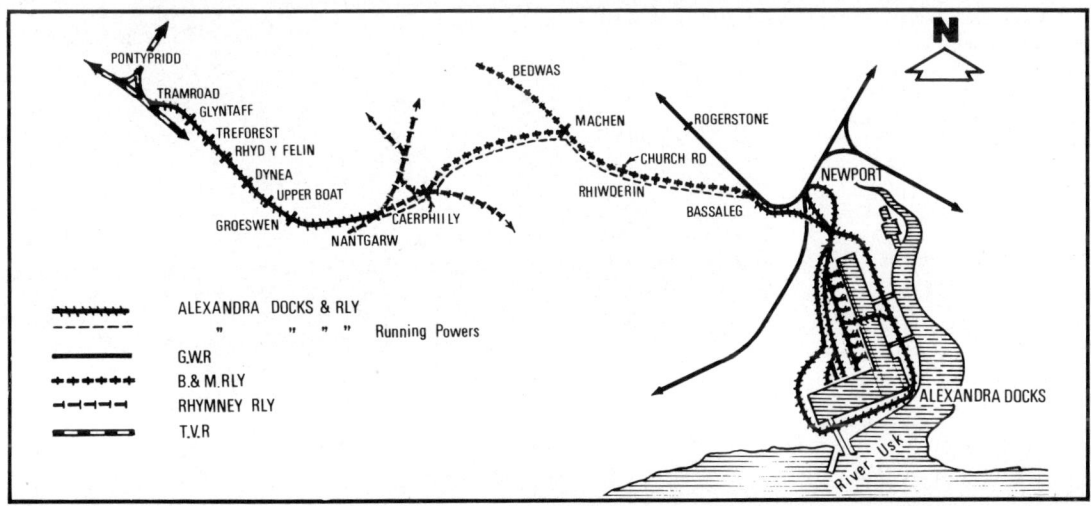

tion where it would connect with its existing dock lines. This new line was brought into use in April 1886. It was hoped that traffic passing over these lines would not be subject to the Tredegar Estates tolls as were the other lines over the Park Mile.

However this hope was not to be and the Tredegar Estates levied its tolls till the GWR bought out the Estates for a sum in excess of £1,000,000 in 1923.

By the Machen Loop Act of 1887 the PC&NR was authorised to double the Caerphilly branch of the B&MR. The new down line was on a diverging route from the original single line (which now became the up line), to give an easier gradient for loaded coal trains than the 1 in 39 they had to face previously. The new up line was brought into use on 14 September 1891 and transferred to the B&MR; in return the B&MR paid the PC&NR 50% of the net earnings of the Caerphilly branch in perpetuity. The ADR absorbed the PC&NR on 31 December 1897.

The ADR had worked a passenger service from the TVR station at Pontypridd to Newport over the PC&NR from 28 December 1887. From 1 January 1899 this service was worked by the GWR until it was withdrawn as an economy measure on 1 January 1917.

As the financial position of the ADR was not good in the earlier half of its life — work was mainly restricted to shunting around the docks — it is not surprising that it tended to purchase mainly second-hand 0-6-0STs. Indeed at the grouping it handed over a very mixed collection of locomotives, quite a large proportion of which were second-hand. Right up to the end of its days the ADR seemed unable to resist a 'bargain'. The result was a stock of engines that must have been a nightmare to the unfortunate storekeeper.

The oldest engine had a most interesting career. It was built for the Metropolitan Railway in 1868 as a 0-6-0T, sold to the Sirhowy Railway in 1873 and taken over by the LNWR who sold it to the ADR in 1891. Named *J. C. Parkinson* and renumbered 26, it was rebuilt to an 0-6-2T by Hawthorne Leslie in 1921, but did not last long after grouping being withdrawn in 1926.

Next came four 0-6-0STs numbered 12, 13, 16 and 17 supplied by Hawthorne Leslie in 1884 and 1889. When No 17 was withdrawn in 1924 its boiler was repaired and fitted to old No 16 in 1927, this enabling No 16 to plod along until withdrawal in 1937. In 1885 R. Stephenson & Co supplied a similar 0-6-0ST. Numbered 15 it was afterwards sold to the Ocean Coal Co and worked at Treharris Colliery until 1947.

Two standard Peckett 0-6-0STs were purchased in 1890-1, numbered 18 and 19, No 18 saw service at Oswestry and Weymouth after the grouping, before being sold for colliery service in 1929. No 19, as GWR No 680, spent the rest of its life working from Oswestry from whence it was withdrawn in 1948.

Right: Railcar No 1, the first of two by the Govan Railway & Engineering Co Ltd. This company was formed by Dugald Drummond when he resigned his position as locomotive superintendent of the Caledonian Railway to take up a position in Australia that failed to materialise.

No 1 drove on one pair of 3ft 0in disc wheels and had seating for 52 passengers. It is seen here on acceptance trials on the ADR in 1904. No 1 lasted in this form until 1917 when the locomotive unit was scrapped and the carriage portion rebuilt into an ordinary carriage with seating for 68 passengers.
Courtesy of National Museum of Wales

Top left: As the railcars were soon found to be lacking in power and accommodation at times of heavy traffic, the ADR purchased three Barnum & Bailey coaches in 1909. These coaches, built on American lines, were part of a train specially built for the circus of Buffalo Bill Cody for his British tour. This train is seen at Pontypridd attached to engine No 28 (former GWR No 1683).
Courtesy of C. W. Harris

Left: No 28 at Machen in 1920 when the ADR was working the passenger service exclusively. No 28 was one of a pair of GWR '1661' class engines purchased by the ADR. Originally intended to be 0-6-0 tender engines, the class was instead built as tank engines with very limited coal capacity, coupled to a 5ft 2in wheel and poor brakes. They were also sold cheaply to the B&MR and Cardiff Railway, and much to their disgust the GWR acquired them again at grouping.
G. H. W. Clifford courtesy C. C. Green

Bottom left: No 14 with a 'standard train' of Barnum & Bailey coaches and a converted railcar trailer drawing up at Rhydyfelin Halt, which was just a sleeper platform at ground level. Most Welsh railways regarded passenger trains as a service to the community that was to be performed as economically as possible.
Courtesy of B. Stevens

9

A further pair of 0-6-0STs — Nos 20 and 21 — were obtained from R. Stephenson & Co in 1894; they were withdrawn in 1925-6. No 21 as GWR No 670 was sold to the Ocean Coal Co and was working at Treorky Colliery until 1947.

In 1903 the ADR dispensed with the services of Messrs Dunn and Shute, who had been contractors at the Town Dock, purchasing from them three small 0-4-0Ts so that the ADR could continue the service as before. Two of these engines were still in service in 1922, unnumbered by the ADR and only known by their names. *Alexandra*, of uncertain origin, was numbered 1341 by the GWR and survived until 1946. The companion engine *Trojan*, was numbered 1340. *Trojan* retained its name in GWR service as the locomotive had brass plates, unlike *Alexandra* whose name was painted on. Sold for industrial service in 1932 *Trojan* worked until purchased for preservation in 1968.

By 1898 the original ex-LNWR 0-6-0STs were in need of replacement so a further pair of 0-6-0STs was purchased from R. Stephenson & Co. Three more were obtained in 1900 — numbered 1 to 5 they turned out to be the largest class of new engines that the ADR ever possessed.

As the Taff Vale Railway intimated that it intended to discontinue working the PC&NR coal trains from 30 April 1903, the ADR decided to work them themselves. Additional locomotives more suitable for main line working became a necessity and once again the ADR was in luck. The Mersey Railway was converting its railway to electric traction and all its steam stud of 2-6-2Ts and 0-6-4Ts was up for sale — the latter being the oldest at just 18 years. The ADR

purchased seven 2-6-2Ts and three 0-6-4Ts in three batches, the last arriving early in 1905. They were stripped of their condensing gear and fitted with cabs before entering service on the coal trains. They proved to be good strong engines, well able to cope with the gradients of the B&MR's Caerphilly branch. After the grouping the GWR did not think much of them; one 2-6-2T was reboilered with a taper boiler in 1923, but to no avail and they were withdrawn, the last in 1931.

Having handed over the PC&NR passenger services to the GWR, the ADR saw a means to boost its revenue by providing a railmotor service to supplement services. In 1904 the first of a pair of railmotors was delivered from the Govan Engineering Co. This company was formed by Dugald Drummond. After resigning his position as Locomotive Superintendent of the Caledonian Railway Drummond took up a post in Australia and when that position failed to materialise, he set up on his own as a manufacturer. The second railmotor from the same source arrived the following year; it was 5ft longer than railmotor No 1 and fitted with a clerestory roof. Like all their breed they were a limited success, having little power in reserve to haul extra coaches. In the end they were converted to ordinary coaches, No 2 in 1911, No 1 in 1917.

In 1906 the ADR made a further excursion into the second-hand market, but this time the company did not get much of a bargain, purchasing two GWR '1661' class 0-6-0STs for £800 each. With their 5ft 2in wheels and an inadequate coal bunker and non-existent brakes, the engines were of dubious value in the docks and filled in on some occasional passenger duties. The GWR managed to unload further engines of the '1661' class on to the B&MR and Cardiff Railway but, much to the GWR's disgust, they all came back at the grouping.

Left: When the TVR informed the ADR that it intended to cease to work the Newport coal trains in 1903, the ADR was able to purchase 10 powerful locomotives from the Mersey Railway. Surplus to requirements since the electrification of that railway, stripped of their condensing gear and fitted with cabs, they were ideal in their new role; here is No 6 (former Mersey No 11) at work in 1920. *G. W. H. Clifford courtesy C. C. Green*

Left: An official photograph of No 29, one of three 0-6-2 saddle tanks built by Andrew Barclay & Co in 1908 for heavy shunting duties on the ADR.
Welsh Railways Research Circle

Below left: No 31 as GWR No 192 after grouping. One of the modifications the GWR carried out was to shorten the saddle tanks. No 192 survived the war and was withdrawn in October 1946. *WRRC*

For heavy shunting duties three 0-6-2STs were supplied by Andrew Barclay; arriving in 1908, they were an instant success. After the grouping, the GWR cut back the saddle tanks so that they no longer covered the smokeboxes. The first one was withdrawn in 1934 but the remaining pair served through World War 2 before they disappeared.

Having decided to replace the railmotors by an engine and coach service, in 1911 the ADR purchased from the GWR a Wolverhampton-built 0-4-2T. Renumbered 14, this locomotive took over the former railmotor duties. It was reboilered before the grouping, but was withdrawn from Malmesbury in 1934.

The Bute Works Supply Co sold the ADR two more ex-GWR engines. The first, in 1912, was originally *Will Scarlet* of the Severn & Wye Railway. An 0-6-0T, the locomotive was withdrawn in 1923. The second engine was a Wolverhampton-built '850' class 0-6-0ST. After the grouping it was rebuilt by the GWR with a pannier tank.

The ADR's last excursion into the second-hand market was in 1919 when two ex-ROD 0-6-0Ts built in 1917 by Kerr Stuart were bought. These two engines proved to be the best of the bargains, though the GWR got most of the benefit. Renumbered 666 and 667 they served until 1955 and 1954 respectively, still at Pill Shed. Much impressed with the performance of the ex-Mersey Railway 2-6-2Ts, the ADR had a pair of 2-6-2Ts built by Hawthorne Leslie in 1920. An updated version of the Mersey engines, they became ADR Nos 36 and 37 remaining at Pill Shed till after World War 2. No 36, as GWR No 1205, was the last to be withdrawn in 1956 — at the same time R. Stephenson & Hawthornes were using the original drawings of the ADR engines to construct locomotives for an Australian colliery.

Though the PC&NR was dependent on the ADR for locomotives to work its passenger trains, it possessed its own coaches. They were built by the Gloucester Carriage & Wagon Co and were identical to coaches that the Metropolitan Carriage & Wagon Co had supplied to the B&MR, indeed, there are grounds for believing that the B&MR lent the drawings to the PC&NR. Additionally in times of stress the

Above: In 1920 the ADR took delivery of two powerful 2-6-2Ts from R. W. Hawthorn; here former ADR No 37, now GWR No 1206 is seen stabled alongside Pill Shed (ADR). This engine was withdrawn in 1951, at the time R. Stephenson & Hawthorn were using the same drawings for an order for an Australian colliery. *WRRC*

ADR hired locomotives and coaches to maintain services from the B&MR. The ADR returned four coaches in 1898 only a few years after it had absorbed the PC&NR. Then in 1904 three ex-Mersey Railway four-wheeled coaches were purchased for strengthening the railmotors and to provide a service when they were out of action. Finally in 1909 the ADR purchased three American style saloons from the Barnum & Bailey circus train that Buffalo Bill Cody had used to tour the country during the early years of the century. These were refitted with longitudinal seating backing beneath the windows and had a capacity of 59 seated. When using these coaches, the ADR formed its trains with a Barnum & Bailey coach coupled to a converted railmotor coach, leaving one Barnum & Bailey coach as a spare. The ex-Mersey Railway coaches were withdrawn from service after World War 1.

The ADR provided a fairly good service over the PC&NR line: there were 10 trips a day with an extra late Saturday night train; the Sunday service consisted of five trips. The ADR services did not work into Pontypridd (TVR) but ter-

minated at their own halt (Tram Road) just short of the PC&NR Junction thus saving any payment to the TVR for junction charges for the railmotor trains. Most of the halts were very rudimentary — just a gate through the boundary fence on to a ground level cinder platform with a name board illuminated by a solitary oil lamp by night. Entry to the train was by means of fixed steps on the former railmotors and Barnum & Bailey coaches.

In 1917 the GWR withdrew the PC&NR Newport-Pontypridd passenger trains as an economy measure. This service had consisted of four trains a day, calling at Caerphilly only en route over the PC&NR after leaving Machen. The ADR extended its own trips to Machen to connect with B&MR trains to compensate — this service superseding the Rhymney Railway's railmotor between Caerphilly and Machen, which the Rhymney Railway withdrew entirely from 5 May 1919. The GWR reintroduced the through trains in 1923 extending them to Merthyr.

The ADR's wagon stock in 1882 consisted of 30 open wagons with an additional 32 on hire. Hired wagons increased in number until in 1891 no less than 548 wagons were on hire. By 1900 the position had changed in that all the hired wagons were taken over and by the Grouping, the ADR handed over 642 open wagons, the majority of these being two and three-plank wagons for internal use in the docks. There were

20 special wagons — ex-Barnum & Bailey bogie flats, built to convey the cages and road vehicles of the circus acts — eight vans and nine goods brake vans. Departmental wagons numbered 13 and included a steam crane.

The ADR had its own workshops in the docks where, besides maintaining the dock plant and machinery, all locomotive and rolling stock repairs were undertaken except for heavy boiler work. Additionally, some of the company's goods stock was built there. The main shed, Pill, was adjacent to the docks; a small shed on the PC&NR line at Glyntaff originally catered for the railmotors, afterwards being the home of the passenger engines.

Below: Groeswen signalbox with permanent way gang in attendance in ADR days. *Courtesy C. Batstone*

In its earlier years the tonnage shipped through the docks did not exceed 500,000 tons, however it continued to increase steadily. Spurred on by the competition of the Barry Railway, the ADR was determined to avoid any congestion or delay at Newport Docks and embarked upon the ambitious South Dock Extension. Opened on 6 June 1893, it was then the largest single dock in the world. With a new lock entrance 1,000ft long and 100ft wide, it opened on 11 July 1914 it was a great asset during World War 1. Unfortunately, the grouping did not allow the ADR to develop it to its true potential.

By 1921 the ADR was shipping over 6,000,000 tons of coal as well as 1,000,000 tons of general traffic. The final dividend of the ADR was $3\frac{1}{2}\%$ on its ordinary shares. It joined the GWR group as a constituent company on 28 March 1922.

The Barry Railway

The first proposal to build a railway and dock at Barry was contained in Acts of Parliament dated 5 July 1865, promoted by persons connected with the Taff Vale Railway. Further Acts were obtained the following year but because of the financial difficulties of 1866 and the limited output of the collieries to be served, no construction ever took place and the acts were abandoned in 1878-9. The Rhondda Coal Owners had become increasingly restive at the reluctance of the Trustees of the Bute Estates to provide improved shipping facilities at Cardiff. The worldwide demand for Welsh steam coal was increasing, but because of the inadequate docks for the ever increasing volume of traffic collieries had to introduce short time working because of the poor turn around of wagons. In 1882 the Bute Estates revived their Parliamentary Bill to build the Roath Dock proposing to increase their already high charges for transhipping at all the Bute Docks by a penny a ton to finance the construction of this long overdue improvement.

This was the final straw as far as the Rhondda Coal Owners and South Wales shipping magnates were concerned. Led by David Davies of the Ocean Colliery Co they proposed to gain Parliamentary powers to build a new dock at Barry with a connecting railway to the Rhondda. The first attempt in 1883 was defeated by the vested interests of the Bute Estates, the Taff Vale and Rhymney Railways. A slightly amended Bill presented the next year was granted on 14 August 1884. The act authorised the construction of a dock at Barry; a railway to Trehafod on the TVR just north of Pontypridd, with a connecting line from Tonteg to the TVR at Treforest; and a line from Drope Junction to the GWR main line at Peterston with an additional link

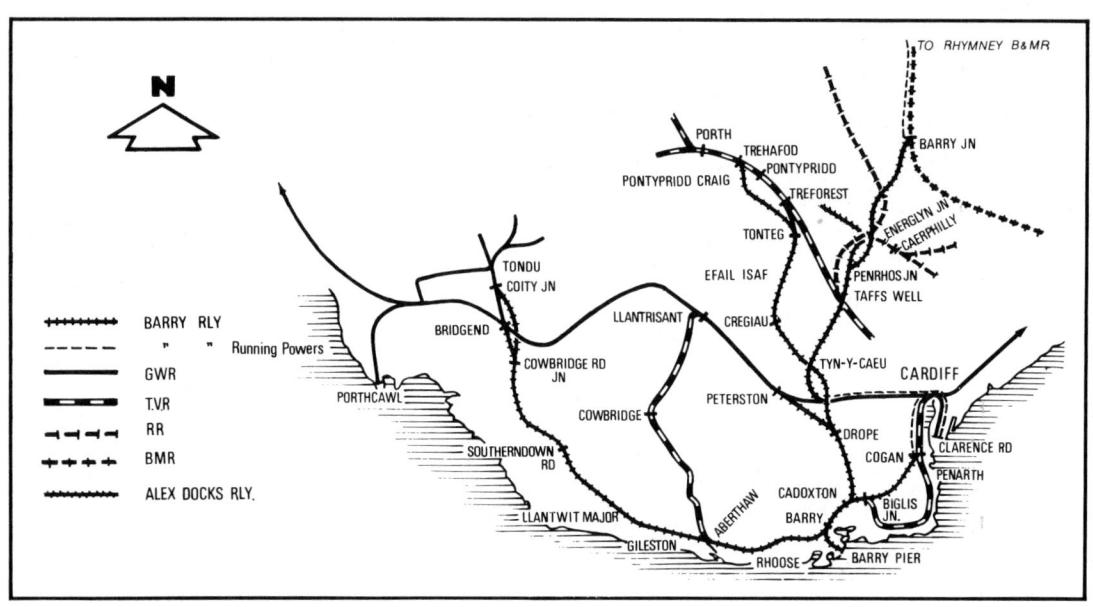

Right: No 72 built by Sharp Stewart in 1895 at work in Barry Docks. No 72 was one of several engines loaned to the GWR in 1917. They worked at Newport, Neath and Dyffryn Yard and did not return home until after the war. *Courtesy C. W. Harris*

Below right:Class B1 No 112 showing the larger tanks that enabled the class to work a train of empty wagons from Cadoxton Yard to Trehafod without stopping for water. The condition of goods engines under H. Golding (Locomotive Superintendent 1905-11) was smarter than many railways of the time. *Courtesy C. W. Harris*

from St Fagans to the Barry Line at Tynycaeau.

In 1885 the TVR attempted to gain powers for a Cardiff, Penarth & Barry Junction Railway, but the company was only partially successful, being authorised to a junction with the Barry Railway at Biglis and further restricted to local traffic only. The Barry Railway's countermove of a Penarth branch was more successful, being authorised to a junction at Cogan on the Penarth branch of the TVR. The Barry Railway was opened for passenger trains only between Cogan Junction and Barry Dock on 20 December 1888; the extension of services to Barry Town station followed on 8 February 1889. Goods trains commenced running between Cogan and Barry on 13 May 1889 — the same day as the main line was opened to the junctions with the GWR at Peterston and St Fagans.

Then the great day dawned, on 18 July 1889 the main line was opened to Trehafod, the dock was opened in front of enthusiastic shareholders and their guests as the first coal trains trundled down from the Rhondda and shipment commenced. The success of the Barry Railway could be gauged at the end of its first full year of operations, when it had carried 3,000,000 tons of coal — despite the TVR cutting its rates aided by generous rebates paid by the Bute Estates.

The Barry Railway began to spread its tentacles in all directions; a bill for a direct line to Cardiff was withdrawn when the TVR granted running powers over its line to the Penarth South junction with the GWR for all classes of traffic. Additionally running powers were granted for goods and mineral trains between Cogan and Taffs Well where traffic from the Rhymney Railway could be tapped. An Act dated 5 August 1891 confirmed these powers; additionally the GWR were compelled to convert their Riverside branch into a passenger line for the benefit of the Barry and Taff Vale Railways. Barry passenger trains were extended from Cogan to the new Riverside station on 14 March 1893. On 2 April 1894 these were further extended to a new terminus at Clarence Road.

As coal exports at Barry topped 4,000,000 tons in 1892 an act was obtained to build the Number 2 Dock at Barry which was opened in 1898.

The development of Barry Island as a pleasure resort was expedited by the construction of the Harbour branch line which was opened on 3 August 1896.

Attempts to build further extensions up the Rhondda valleys were unsuccessful, though on 16 March 1896 powers were granted to extend its passenger trains from Barry to Porth where connections were made with trains off the Rhondda Fach and Fawr branches.

a wheelbase of only 12ft and only weighing $27\frac{1}{2}$ tons — a very useful and neat engine. In 1909, when the then Locomotive Superintendent H. Golding was experimenting with a railmotor train, he had No 33 into the works. The engine emerged in full passenger livery with the rear couping rods removed, which turned it into an 0-4-2T No 33 worked over the Vale of Glamorgan line in this state until J. Auld (the last Locomotive Superintendent of the Barry Railway) abandoned railmotor trains and restored the coupling rods.

As an improved engine for heavy shunting, J. Hosgood ordered a saddle tank version of the 'A' class. Designated Class F the class eventually comprised 28 engines that proved their worth in Barry docks with its ever increasing volume of traffic. During World War 1 some of them were loaned to the GWR.

Preparatory to the opening of the Vale of Glamorgan line, the first 0-8-2Ts in Britain were delivered by Sharp Stewart in 1896. These seven engines were intended for heavy coal trains from the Llynfi and Ogmore valleys. This never materialised — in fact the traffic that did pass was within the capacity of the 'B1' engines. So the 'H' class, as the 0-8-2Ts were known, were put to hauling 100-wagon coal trips from Cadoxton to Barry Docks.

At the end of the last century, British locomotive builders had full order books and could not accept any more orders for immediate delivery. The Barry Railway urgently required more 'B1' engines, and was forced to go to the USA and placed an order with the Cooke Locomotive Co of New Jersey in 1899. With American bar frames, outside cylinders and a drumhead smokebox, the remainder of the design was standard Barry practice. Delivered in parts the engines were assembled at Barry. They were found to be heavier on coal and water than British-built 'B1s' so they were sent to Trehafod and took over the bank engine duties there. After experimenting with extended smokeboxes, they were eventually reboilered with standard Barry boilers.

Below: After the arrival of more 'B1s' they took over most of the main line workings from the 'H' class all of which were transferred to 100-wagon coal trips from Cadoxton Yard and the Docks. No 84 is seen here at Cadoxton on these duties. *Courtesy C. W. Harris*

Left, top to bottom: The 'D' class was the first modern 0-8-0 tender engine in the country built by Sharp Stewart in 1888 for the Swedish & Norwegian Railway. Unfortunately this company could not afford them and the Barry Railway purchased two in 1889 and a further two in 1897. Here is No 35 of the first pair after reboilering in 1901, seen at Cadoxton where it worked trips to Penarth and Docks in turn with the 0-8-2T. *Courtesy C. W. Harris*

No 93 of the second pair with an unaltered cab; this pair usually worked trips between Cadoxton and New Tredegar on the B&MR. A small class of four engines, the 'D' class did not find favour with the GWR and all were gone by 1930. *Courtesy C. W. Harris*

In 1899 no British manufacturer could supply locomotives to satisfy the Barry Railway with its ever increasing traffic. So an order was placed with the Cooke Loco Co of New Jersey USA. Based on the successful 'B1' they had bar frames, outside cylinders with a drumhead smokebox. No 120 of Class K, as the Barry classified them, is as supplied by the maker. *WRRC*

For light shunting over very sharp curves the little Class E 0-6-0Ts were ideal. No 34 of 1889, renumbered 782 by the GWR is seen here at Barry in 1924. Sold out of service in 1939, No 782 survived in colliery service until 1958. *WRRC*

19

The first passenger engines were four small 2-4-0Ts supplied by Sharp Stewart in 1889-90. While adequate for the initial service from Cogan to Barry, when this service was extended to Cardiff and expanded they had inadequate water and coal for the heavier trains. In 1897 they were taken out of service and during the next year Nos 21 and 22 were rebuilt as 2-4-2Ts at Barry. No 37 was sold to the Port Talbot Railway the same year. That company also purchased the last one, No 52, but she was rebuilt as a 2-4-2T before departing from Barry. Nos 21 and 22 gravitated to the lighter Vale of Glamorgan trains where they replaced the experimental railmotor working.

To replace the 'C' class the Vulcan Foundry supplied a pair of 0-4-4Ts; a second pair arrived from Sharp Stewart in 1895. Known as Class G, they worked the Cardiff branch passenger trains until the increasing weight of these trains overtaxed their capabilities. When the railmotors proved to be inadequate on the Cardiff-Pontypridd via St Fagans trains, the 'G's took over. Their rapid acceleration from stops with these lighter trains helped them to be excellent time keepers.

The final class of passenger engines were the 'J' class 2-4-2T. The first three from Hudswell Clarke arrived in 1897, the remainder from Sharp Stewart in 1898-99. They took over the heavier

Above: In 1909 Mr Golding gave No 33 full passenger livery and removed the rear coupling rods and fitted it for auto-working between Barry and the Vale of Glamorgan line. J. Auld, the last Locomotive Superintendent of the Barry Railway, disconnected the auto-gear and restored the coupling rods, but these workings continued as engine and coaches till grouping. *WRRC*

trains from the earlier engines where their greater coal and water capacity was a decided advantage. All Barry engines were clean but the finish of a 'J' class for a normal day's work would have put many a main line company to shame. Unfortunately after grouping they were displaced by the GWR '39xx' class 2-6-2Ts.

J. Auld only ordered one class of engine after he took office, the 10 engines of the 'L' class of 0-6-4Ts supplied by Hawthorn Leslie in 1914. Called mixed traffic engines they did not do much passenger work as a rule. Normally they were rostered for main line coal trains where they were often in trouble because of an incurable tendency for the trailing bogie to derail on yard and siding points. The GWR rebuilt four of them with taper boilers in 1923. Laid aside during the 1926 General Strike, they never returned to traffic. The whole class was cut up at Swindon the same year — and when it came to light that they were only 12 years old, Swindon had to answer some awkward questions!

Left: For the initial passenger trains between Barry Town and Cogan the Barry Railway had four small 2-4-0Ts. Their small coal and water capacity was a disadvantage, when services were extended to Cardiff, so three were rebuilt as 2-4-2Ts, though subsequently one of the rebuilds and the remaining 2-4-0T were sold to the PTR in 1898. No 22 as rebuilt is seen here in 1920 attached to a former Lancashire & Yorkshire Railway brake third. Three 10-coach trains were purchased from the L&YR in 1916 when coaches were urgently required.
G. H. W. Clifford courtesy of C. C. Green

Below left: To replace the 'Cs' on the expanding passenger services, the Barry purchased four 0-4-4Ts. These worked on the Barry-Cardiff services until the more powerful Class Js arrived on the scene. Here is No 67 on a Pontypridd train at Cardiff Riverside station.
G. H. W. Clifford courtesy C. C. Green

Bottom left: The Class G, as the 0-4-4Ts were designated, took over the Cardiff-Pontypridd and Barry-Pontypridd trains from the railmotor cars; on these routes their faster running with a lighter train was appreciated. No 69 is alongside Barry shed in 1920. *WRRC*

Left, top to bottom: After the grouping the GWR soon scrapped the 0-4-4s because it didn't like the wheel arrangement. However No 66 was photographed on Barry shed as GWR No 2 in 1925. *WRRC*

No 89 of the second batch of Class Js, built in 1898 outside Barry shed after attention by the cleaners. With the crimson livery of the Barry Railway they must have been a magnificent sight. *Courtesy of C. W. Harris*

The last engine of Class J, No 98 is on a Cardiff-Barry train in 1920 at Cardiff (Riverside) station. *G. H. W. Clifford courtesy of C. C. Green*

John Auld during his term of office only introduced one class of engine, the Class L 0-6-4T in 1914. This class of 10 engines, though classed as mixed traffic, did little passenger work, the 2-4-2T being preferred. Except for a tendency for the bogies to derail on yard points they proved a strong reliable engine. Here No 141 works a passenger train from Cardiff (Riverside) in 1920. *G. H. W. Clifford courtesy of C. C. Green*

Top right: The Barry Railway purchased two railmotor cars in 1905 from the North British Loco Co who subcontracted the coachwork to R. Y. Pickering. Intended for the Cardiff-Pontypridd service were soon found to have insufficient power, so they were utilised on the Barry Island and Vale of Glamorgan relief trains. Car No 2 is seen here outside the Barry's own little railmotor shed at Barry. *Courtesy of National Museum of Wales.*

Following the trends of the times the Barry Railway purchased two steam rail motors from the North British Locomotive Co in 1905. Very similar to contemporary GWR railmotors they were intended to work between Pontypridd and Cardiff via St Fagans. Unfortunately they had great difficulty in surmounting the climb from St Fagans to Tynycaeau Junction and had to be relegated to short trips over the Vale of Glamorgan line and a summer shuttle service between Barry station and Barry Island. When their boilers required renewing in 1910, the engine units were scrapped and the car bodies rebuilt as composite coaches. After the grouping the GWR converted them into auto train trailers.

Passenger trains commenced with 22 four-wheeled coaches supplied by the Metropolitan Carriage & Wagon Co, added to as traffic increased. The first six-wheeled coaches arrived in 1895, being made up into 10-coach trains for the Cardiff Branch; Pontypridd trains were usually five-coach sets. The four-wheeled coaches were gradually downgraded to colliers trains and for coal trimmers to travel in. The only venture into the second-hand market was the purchase in 1916 of 30 coaches from the Lancashire & York-shire Railway. The last additions to stock in 1920 were two seven-coach sets of bogie coaches from the Birmingham Carriage & Wagon Co; with

flush sides and high pitched roofs, they were very up to date for their day. The Barry relied on the old fashioned foot warmers to keep their passengers happy during the winter months yet they fitted electric lights to all their coaching stock including the four-wheelers. The brake vans were fitted with electric tail and side lights — these were removed by the GWR and replaced with oil lamps in the name of uniformity.

The Cardiff branch had an intense service of 25 trains a day on weekdays with 11 on Sundays. The main line to Pontypridd and Porth had five or six trains on weekdays with three on Sundays, while the Cardiff to Pontypridd service via St Fagans was more ambitious with 10 trains on weekdays and four on Sundays. The Vale of Glamorgan line had seven trains on weekdays with additional trips to Llantwit Major; Sunday travellers had three trains either way.

The wayside stations of the main line were of a pleasing appearance built of dressed stone, while the Barry and Cardiff branch stations were invariably wooden clap-boarded structures. In contrast the Vale of Glamorgan line stations were commodious brick buildings that were very lavish considering the traffic that they dealt with.

The goods stock handed over at grouping comprised 693 open wagons, 752 vans, and 118 timber and cattle wagons. The 70 goods brake vans were mostly vacuum-piped so that they could be attached to passenger trains and at the end of a journey the coach set could be detached while the engine, van and guard would soon be working another coal train to Barry. The large number of vans was required to convey flour from Joseph Rank's mill at the docks.

The Barry Pier branch was opened for the summer services of 1899 and Bristol Channel pleasure steamers started to call for excursion traffic. The Barry Railway applied for powers to run steamers between Barry and various Somerset and Devon ports. Initially the application was refused because of the opposition of other railway and steamboat companies. As the number of passengers became greater than the steamboat companies could cater for, a second application was granted by an act dated 1904. Unfortunately there were so many restrictions in the act that it was of little practical value. The Barry Company could not engage in local coastal general cargo trade and only passengers and their luggage were to be carried between Barry, West-super-Mare and Ilfracombe. Summer excursions were allowed between Bristol and Tenby but they had to terminate at Barry and only passengers who had made the outward journey from Barry were allowed to be carried on the return trips. Two paddle steamers were purchased new for the service which commenced in 1905, two additional steamers were obtained in 1907. While the number of passengers carried was encouraging the service was always unprofitable. An attempt to transfer the steamers to a nominally independent company to avoid the Parliamentary restrictions led to disputes and had to be dropped. Finally in 1910 the steamers were sold at a loss. This proved to be the only venture by the Barry Railway on which they failed to show a profit.

Like most Welsh railways somersault signals were adopted, though the Barry Railway used Saxby & Farmer as signalling contractors. The later renewals had pressed steel enamelled arms with two white bands. Some of these later signals lasted until the end of services under British Railways. Tyers two-position one-wire block instruments were normal, though on some of the more heavily trafficked sections Tyers three-position instruments had been installed.

The permanent way, though of the latest heavy section rails, always retained the outmoded

method of being keyed on the inside of the rails.

The Barry Railway in 1913 shipped 11,000,000 tons of coal through Barry Docks — this by a railway that only had two small collieries directly connected to its system. In its final year of independence, notwithstanding a major coal strike, 5,500,000 tons of coal were shipped as well as nearly 3,000,000 passengers carried. The lucky shareholders regularly received 10% dividends on their ordinary shares.

The Barry Railway held out against the original grouping proposals by which all Welsh Companies were to be absorbed by the GWR. It was abhorrent to the railway to suggest that a successful company, which could regularly pay dividends of 10%, should be absorbed by a company that had never managed to pay more than 7½%, and that on infrequent occasions. With great reluctance, after a brief life of 38 years during which so much had been accomplished, the Barry Railway joined the GWR group as a constituent company on 5 April 1922.

Left: No 144 arrives in Cadoxton Yard with a coal train, one of the 'L' class's usual duties. The smokebox door numberplates instead of the usual brass numerals on the chimney and other details made them distinctively different from the rest of the Barry Railway locomotives. *WRRC*

Below left: The Barry Railway opened a shed at Coity Junction, Bridgend in anticipation of traffic that did not materialise. This photograph shows staff and 'B1' No 39 at Coity Shed before the Barry Railway reduced it to a coaling and watering point only, in 1906. *Courtesy H. T. Hobbs*

Right, top to bottom: A Vale of Glamorgan line train leaving Barry Town behind 'B1' No 60 in 1921; note the signal gantry fitted with the latest steel signal arms with twin black bands. Some of these signals lasted in certain spots until the majority of the Barry main line was closed by British Railways. *Courtesy of B. Stevens*

Barry Island at the same period, built to cater for the expanding excursion traffic; note the scissors crossover in the foreground, installed to facilitate engine changing. *Courtesy B. Stevens*

Creigiau station in 1922 in its placid rural setting that seemed to be far removed from traffic like coal trains. *Courtesy B. Stevens*

Llantwit Major on the Vale of Glamorgan line; the through middle roads were installed so that coal trains could have an unbroken trip and overtake intermediate passenger trains. *Courtesy of Lens of Sutton*

The Brecon & Merthyr Tydfil Railway

The Brecon & Merthyr, as it was usually known, was incorporated by two Acts of Parliament dated 1 August 1859 and 15 May 1860 to build a railway over the heavy gradients between the Vale of Usk and the Taff Fechan. It was hoped that with a better means of communication than the existing Abergavenny & Brecon Canal and the Brinore Tramroad, the produce of agricultural Brecknock could find a market in the rapidly expanding towns of Dowlais and Merthyr. In return the cost of iron, coal and lime would be greatly reduced in Brecknock.

Unfortunately even before construction commenced there were serious differences with other embryo railways, principally the Hereford, Hay & Brecon and the Mid Wales Railways. This led to the promotion of conflicting bills as each company attempted to counter its opponents' aspirations. However, the expertise that the B&MR acquired in this expensive form of skirmishing was to stand it in good stead in the years ahead.

The contractors for the first sections of the B&MR were David Davies, Thomas Savin and John Ward. Davies soon dropped out of the partnership because of differences with Savin over other railway contracts that they were engaged upon. This left Savin and his brother-in-law Ward to complete the initial contracts successfully.

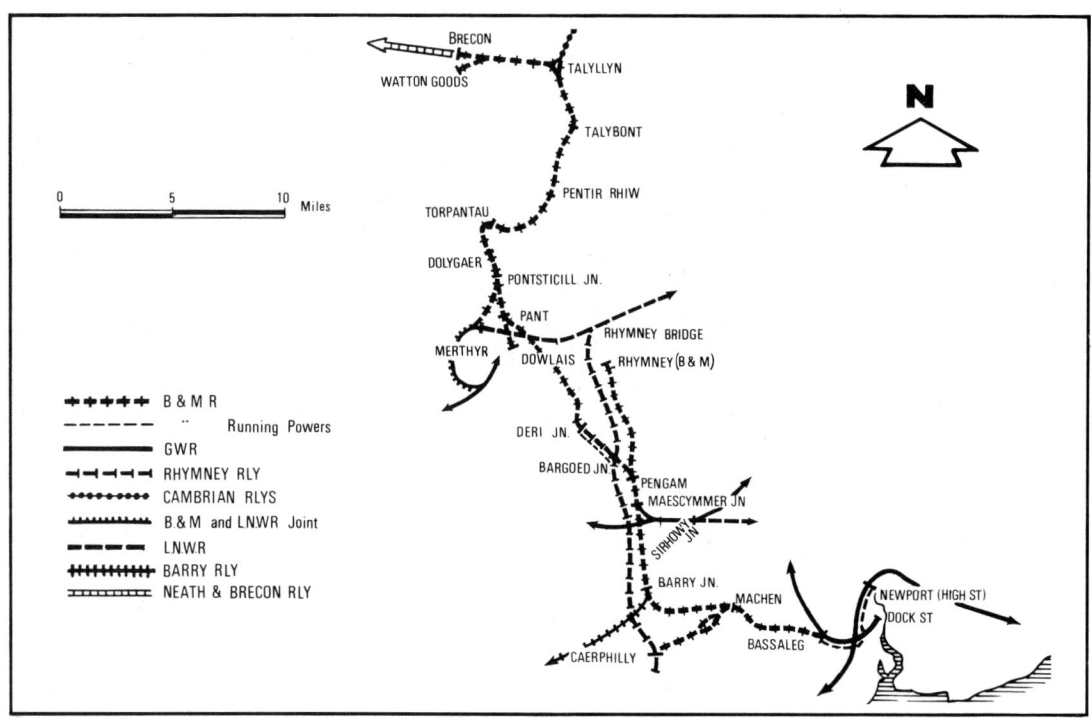

There were delays in resolving differences with the HH&BR and Mid Wales Railway over the purchase of the Hay Tramroad, which the three companies wanted to acquire to convert its trackbed into a railway line into the county town of Brecon. But on 1 May 1863 the first passenger train steamed into Brecon from Pant to a temporary terminus at the Watton.

The second entrant into Brecon was the Mid Wales Railway which began running goods and passenger trains to Brecon on 21 September 1864; on the same day the East Loop at Talyllyn was brought into use. The Hereford, Hay & Brecon Railway having spurned the West Midland Railway, had fallen on hard times and T. Savin took over the contract to build it. Additionally he contracted to work the train services which ran through to Brecon in September 1864. An act to amalgamate the B&MR and the HH&BR was granted on 5 July 1865. This was the end of the Neath & Brecon's hopes to connect with the HH&BR and the N&BR agreed to a junction to the east of Mount Street, 12 chains west of the new Free Street passenger station that the B&MR was building for the use of all companies.

As a result of an investigation into the affairs of the B&MR following the financial crisis of 1866, it was discovered that the Amalgamation Act was illegal as it had never been approved by the debenture share holders; so the two companies resumed their separate status by the B&MR Agreement Act of 1868.

Brecon Free Street was opened on 1 March 1871, and initially was only used by the trains of the B&MR and HH&BR. The Mid Wales trains which had been enjoying the hospitality of the N&BR at Mount Street began to use Free Street from 1 May 1871, leaving the N&BR in solitary isolation at Mount Street until 1874 when it agreed to extend its trains to Free Street.

Below: These Sharp Stewart 0-6-0STs gave good service to the end. Being fairly powerful with a short wheelbase, nine of them were sold to industrial companies on withdrawal. Here is former B&MR No 27 *Hercules* at work for the Ebbw Vale Steel, Iron & Coal Co; it had been withdrawn from the BMR in 1899.
Courtesy National Museum of Wales

Right: In 1881 the B&MR took delivery of two small 0-6-0ST engines to replace the original tender engines on the Newport passenger trains. Despite their small wheels of 4ft 7in diameter, they were capable of keeping time. Here is No 18 on this work before the end of the last century. *Courtesy C. C. Green*

Centre right: After being displaced from the main line in the early years of this century, 0-6-0Ts, graduated to the Dowlais branch where they lasted till after grouping performing all duties. Here is No 17 on Dowlais branch duty at Pant in 1905. *Courtesy C. C. Green*

Bottom right: No 18 at Dowlais just before grouping — soon after takeover by the GWR the engine went to Swindon Works for heavy repairs, emerging with pannier tanks, and a spark arresting chimney; it then worked in Didcot Ordnance Depot till May 1934.
Courtesy E. W. Hannan

In 1863 T. Savin contracted to lease the B&MR for 10 years, to supply locomotives and rolling stock, run all services and pay the shareholders 5% interest on all fully paid up shares.

The ambitions of the B&MR were limitless; it was now promoting acts that would enable it to build its own railways to Newport, Cardiff and Nantybwlch at the last point it wished to connect with the Merthyr, Tredegar & Abergavenny Railway making it unnecessary for that railway to extend itself any further westwards.

The Taff Vale and the Rhymney Railways were now incensed by the expansionist tactics of the B&MR. The TVR successfully petitioned to have a restricting clause in the B&MR's Bargoed-Rhymney Branch Act, thus preventing the B&MR from opening this railway until it had completed it original line to Merthyr.

Next the B&MR purchased the 'Rumney Tramroad', opened in 1825, which ran for the Rhymney Ironworks down the valley, and then turned eastwards to Machen and Bassaleg, where it connected with the Sirhowy and Park Mile Tramroads of the Tredegar Estates and gained access to Newport Dock. The 'Rumney Tramroad' had powers under an Act of Parliament dated 1 August 1861, to convert its tramroad into a railway, to run passenger services and to build a branch line from Machen to Caerphilly to connect with the Rhymney Railway. The B&MR took over the 'Rumney Tramroad' on 28 July 1863 and immediately commenced to carry out the conversion works. The GWR, as successors to the West Midland Railway, opened its connecting junction at Maescymmer on 28 December 1863 and exercised its inherited running powers over the former 'Rumney Tramroad' for traffic other than that consigned to a Bristol Channel port. The B&MR completed the conversion of the tramroad and passenger trains started between Pengam and Dock Street Newport on 18 June 1865: Dock Street was the terminus of the Monmouthshire Railway & Canal Co. Passenger trains were extended to Rhymney on 16 August 1866, the Caerphilly branch having been opened as a mineral line in 1864.

As both the B&MR and Rhymney's acts authorised the construction of both lines over the same stretch of the Rhymney Valley at Bargoed, a whole new source of contention arose as the B&MR striving to block LNWR and Rhymney parliamentary bills. Eventually a compromise was reached: the Rhymney was to build between Bargoed and Deri Junction, while the B&MR was to build between Dowlais Top and Deri. The B&MR was to have running powers for its through traffic, in return the Rhymney was allowed to work up to the collieries at Fochriw.

Now the troubles of the B&MR were beginning to emerge: Savin had overcommitted himself, with many of his contracts paid in preference shares and little cash. Also had had become hopelessly involved in speculative hotels and boarding house projects at Borth and Aberystwyth that had proved to be little more than 'white elephants'. The result was that he was unable to pay the guaranteed dividend from 5 February 1866.

An even worse disaster occurred on 'Black Friday', 10 May 1866, when the Quaker bankers Overend and Gurney, who specialised in railway finance, failed with liabilities of £11,000,000. This catastrophe caused problems for some of the largest railways in the country. The immediate effect on the B&MR was the cessation of all construction work on the Merthyr line, leaving the Cefn Coed viaduct unfinished.

Hopelessly overextended, the B&MR failed to pay debenture share interest and its creditors had a Receiver appointed by the Chancery Court. Sorting out the problem took two years hard work and culminated in the B&MR Arrangement Act, dated 13 July 1868, that reorganised the company's debts as additional debenture shares.

Unable to open a direct Brecon-Newport service until it had completed its line to Merthyr, Alexander Sunderland (the B&MR's engineer) took over the unfinished Merthyr contract, com-

Above: No 12, one of the second pair of passenger engines, at Newport. With their gleaming brass domes and burnished steelwork coupled to the red brown colour these engines were certainly a sight to catch the eye. *WRRC*

pleting the Cefn Coed Viaduct. Train services were extended to Cefn on 1 August 1867. After completion to Rhydycar Junction, running powers over the Vale of the Neath line to Merthyr High Street station enabled passenger trains finally to reach Merthyr from Brecon on 1 August 1868. The B&MR lost no time in commencing its Newport-Brecon services — they started a month later on 1 September 1868. After the GWR took over the Monmouthshire Railway they constructed the Gaer Loop Line which enabled them to divert all passenger trains from Dock Street to the High Street station from 11 March 1880.

As an alternative to its original proposal to gain access to Dowlais by running over the lines of the Dowlais Ironworks, the B&MR opened its branch from Pant to a terminus at Lloyd Street Dowlais on 23 June 1869.

The separate existence of the B&MR nearly terminated in 1874 when the Midland Railway and the Monmouthshire Railway promoted a bill to acquire the B&MR. The directors and shareholders accepted, but the debenture shareholders petitioned against the bill as it virtually ignored their prior claims on the B&MR. The Midland withdrew the bill, thus sounding the death knell for the Act, and also for that company's hopes of having its own route to Newport and Cardiff.

So the B&MR struggled along, trying to generate traffic over its system. The Northern

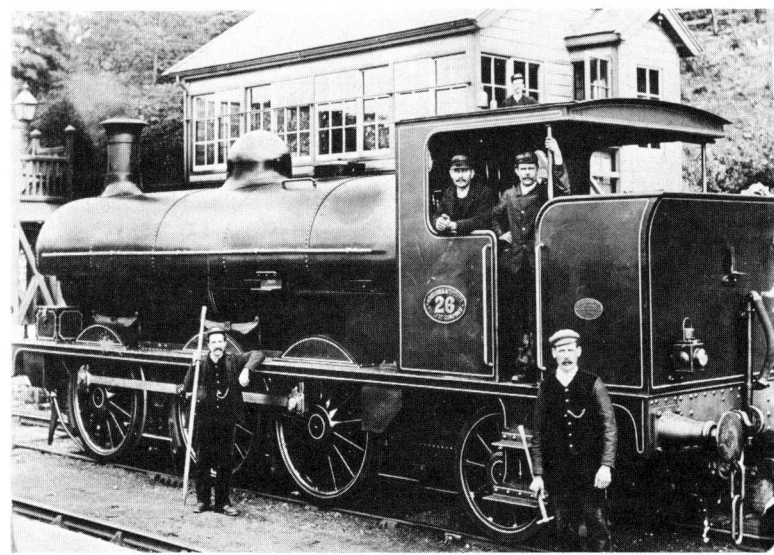

Right: A larger edition of the Sharp Stewart 0-6-0ST was obtained from the Vulcan Foundry in 1894, now of the 0-6-2 wheel arrangement. Though nominally goods engines, they did a fair amount of passenger workings in the Northern Division. In fact, when the B&MR was called upon to work a Royal Train on 27 June 1896, Nos 23 and 26 of this class double-headed it between Talyllyn over the hills and Merthyr where it was handed over to the TVR — one of the few occasions that goods engines have undertaken such exalted duties. Here No 26 is at Pontsticill Junction in 1896 with driver John Davies in charge. *Courtesy of Breconshire Railway Society*

Right: Brecon station before World War 1 with the afternoon passenger train that was double-headed to Pontsticill where it would be split into separate trains for Merthyr and Newport. As the driver of the leading engine is Ben Watkins it is probably his regular engine, No 23 an 0-6-2ST, double-heading a 2-4-0T. *Courtesy of Breconshire Railway Society*

section, with its heavy gradients and agricultural background, was not very encouraging, but the Southern section — centred on the Rhymney Valley with its iron works and collieries and easier gradients — gave a glimmer of hope for the future.

Though money was short, the B&MR could always engage in litigation. This little railway continued to war with the GWR, LNWR and the Midland as well as with the other Welsh railways, for what it believed were its rights. Somehow it usually managed to emerge from each encounter slightly better off than its opponents. It successfully denied access to Brecon from the Vale of Crickhowell, undoubtedly the only logical route. Perhaps its crest — the twin shields of Brecknock and Glamorgan — inspired it: the bats on the shield of Brecknock were portrayed as bees on

the B&MR device. Napoleon Bonaparte also had bees on his coat of arms; perhaps the B&MR inherited his warlike qualities? The motto *Per Adua Facile*, 'through difficulties with ease', it certainly lived up to.

The Barry Railway gained access to the Rhymney branch by its extension line from Penrhos Junction opened on 2 January 1905. The Barry Railway worked only coal trains, though excursion trains to Barry Island were run from the Rhymney Valley by this route. Though the B&MR lost a certain amount of coal traffic that was diverted from Newport to Barry Docks, it was well compensated by its receipts from the passage of traffic off the Rhymney Railway that the Barry Railway syphoned away from its former route to Cardiff. Additionally the Barry Railway provided most of the money to pay for the doubling of the B&MR up to Abertysswg and the cost of installing additional signalboxes to avoid delays to B&MR trains.

With the expansion of the collieries connected to its system, by the end of the first decade of this century money was made available for more modern locomotives and additional rolling stock, and the track had been relaid with 80lbs and 90lb rails. In 1913 3,500,000 tons of coal were carried, and 2,000,000 passenger journeys were made. The interest was paid in full on all preference and debenture shares, only the poor holders of the ordinary stock were without a dividend. As these were only £225,000 out of a total capital of £2,000,000, this was better than it appeared.

After the fiasco of Savin and Ward working the railway by contract, the B&MR took over a very mixed collection of locomotives that were 'found' in various locations on other railways also

worked by Savin. Some locomotives that they inherited were found to belong to other companies and had to be surrendered.

The B&MR's share turned out to be five standard Sharp Stewart 0-6-0 tender engines, with a very similar engine by Manning Wardle; two 2-4-0 passenger tender engines; two 0-4-2 mixed traffic engines, also by Sharp Stewart; and a pair of old 0-6-0 engines by Slaughter & Grunning. The tank engines consisted of two 0-6-0STs built by Sharp Stewart, and three Manning Wardle small 0-6-0STs. Luckily Savin had ordered from Sharp Stewart six long-boilered 0-6-0STs that took over the goods workings at the Brecon end of the line. A further six enlarged engines of this type were delivered in 1870-2.

The two double-framed 0-6-0STs purchased from the Neath & Brecon Railway in 1877 were named *Allt* and *Tor* and were the last named

Above left: During the early years of this century as the financial position improved, the B&MR ordered 0-6-2Ts based on the Rhymney Railway Class R, the drawings of which were borrowed. A class of eight engines was built up over five years. No 37 was originally allocated to Brecon and is seen here with driver Ted Burnett and staff before being reallocated to Bassaleg shed in 1913. *Courtesy D. Pullen*

Left: Further engines of a larger wheel diameter were ordered during World War 1 but not delivered until 1921. Though classed as mixed traffic engines they went straight on to passenger workings. Here is No 48 halted at Pant in 1922. *WRRC*

31

engines on the B&MR. They are believed to be the first to carry numberplates, and about the same time bufferbeam numbers were introduced.

As replacements for the 2-4-0 tender engines on the Newport-Brecon passenger trains, two small saddle tanks were supplied by Sharp Stewart in 1881. With wheels of only 4ft 7in diameter they coped with these trains successfully until displaced by the 2-4-0T engines, the first of which arrived in 1888, with coupled wheels of 5ft 0in diameter. Ultimately a class of six they took over the principal passenger trains until they were displaced after the grouping.

Much impressed by the performance of the two ex-N&BR 0-6-0STs, a class of 12 similar engines was obtained from R. Stephenson and J. Fowler between 1884 and 1886. On their arrival all the old Savin tender engines were withdrawn.

Six similar 0-6-0STs, but with full length saddle tanks and an over cab enclosing the coal bunkers, arrived between 1896 and 1900 to replace the old Sharp Stewart long-boilered saddle tanks which were proving inadequate for the increasing loads. However the B&MR took delivery of a pair of long-boilered 0-6-2STs in 1894, followed by a further pair in 1905. This enlarged version proved to be very useful and did a lot of passenger work on the Northern section. In fact when the B&MR had to provide power for a Royal Train between Talyllyn and Merthyr in 1896, Nos 23 and 26 double-headed the Royal Train over the B&MR. What a sight they must have presented in their gleaming chocolate livery! Between 1906 and 1907 the B&MR purchased three GWR '1661' class 0-6-0STs. With their limited coal capacity and poor brakes, they were mostly to be seen in Bassaleg yard or on an occasional trip up the Rhymney Valley.

An even more unsuitable GWR 'bargain' arrived in 1908 — former GWR No 1490 was purchased from the Ebbw Vale Steel, Iron & Coal Co and was employed mostly on Rhymney colliers trains until sold to the Cramlingham Colliery in 1916.

Developing traffic and the easing of the purse strings enabled the first modern 0-6-2Ts to be ordered. Based on the Rhymney Railways Class M; eight of these engines were delivered between 1909 and 1914. After the grouping they were rebuilt with Rhymney Belpaire boilers and they were all still in service at nationalisation.

In 1914 an ex-LSWR 4-4-2T was purchased. Unfortunately its 5ft 6in driving wheels were a handicap on the main line so it was transferred to the Rhymney branch.

The last class of B&MR engines was of the 0-6-2T type, had 5ft 0in coupled wheels and was designated for mixed traffic. The first three were delivered in 1915 but because of wartime shortages the final trio were not delivered until 1921. Again, all were still steaming along at nationalisation.

The final B&MR venture in the second-hand market was the purchase of an ex-ROD 0-6-0T of Kerr Stuart 'Victory' class, identical to the pair the ADR purchased.

The original coaches of the B&MR were supplied by W. Adams of Birmingham who had become one of the earliest suppliers of rolling stock on hire purchase terms. They comprised 40 four-wheeled coaches that carried passengers with few additions and replacements for many

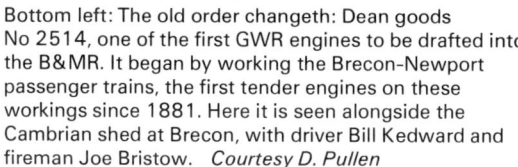

Bottom left: The old order changeth: Dean goods No 2514, one of the first GWR engines to be drafted into the B&MR. It began by working the Brecon-Newport passenger trains, the first tender engines on these workings since 1881. Here it is seen alongside the Cambrian shed at Brecon, with driver Bill Kedward and fireman Joe Bristow. *Courtesy D. Pullen*

Above: The 'Foundry' Machen, the locomotive, carriage and wagon shops of the B&MR. Originally erected by the old 'Rhumney Tramroad', the main line originally ran between the two lines of workshops. It was closed by the GWR on 19 March 1927 when work and staff were transferred to the enlarged Caerphilly Works. *Courtesy of W. A. Camwell*

Right, top to bottom: Seen in early GWR days, Machen Junction signalbox controlled the junction to Caerphilly branch and the exchange sidings. The B&M&R built several of its larger signalboxes to this pattern. *WRRC*

The Rhymney branch was troubled by slips and subsidences several times, culminating in the 1905 temporary closure — on this occasion extensive damage was caused to the adjacent colliery. The final slip of 1930 was of such magnitude that the railway and adjoining road were engulfed while the colliery shafts were so distorted that they had to be realigned. *Courtesy P. Korrison*

Ivor Junction, Dowlais had the largest signal gantry on the B&MR. It controlled points leading to the world famous Dowlais Iron Co which was taken over in later years by Guest, Keen & Nettlefolds. A cabless saddle tank loco of GKN is on the siding to the right. *Courtesy B. Stevens*

Pontsticill Junction in 1921 with a Merthyr branch goods train about to leave. *Courtesy B. Stevens*

Left: Merthyr GWR with its original Brunel shed as built for the Vale of Neath Railway. A B&MR passenger train for Pontsticill Junction is just leaving in the centre. On the right is a Rhymney Railway train for Cardiff running over the RR-GWR Joint line. Merthyr station was also used by the TVR and LNWR trains daily, and during some summers the Cambrian Railways also worked the Aberystwyth-Cardiff holiday trains through to Merthyr. *Courtesy B. Stevens*

Centre left: Talybont on Usk looking 'down line' (Welsh railway somewhat logically worked down towards the coast), showing the foot of the notorious seven-mile bank — $6\frac{1}{2}$ miles of 1 in 38 and half a mile of 1 in 68 terminating in a 650yd tunnel. *Courtesy P. Korrison*

years. In fact by 1900 they had only risen to 55 coaches, but as finances improved a fresh source of supply presented itself. Various railways were carrying out electrification projects, so from 1903 the B&MR acquired coaches from the Mersey, Metropolitan, LSWR and Midland Railways at very reasonable prices. Most of this stock was far more comfortable than the usual spartan nature of B&M upholstery and, additionally, some of the ex-LSWR stock was electrically lit.

The usual B&MR train formation was a six-coach set, with two full brakes outermost, three

Above: Talyllyn station looking towards Brecon showing the tunnel entrance. The tunnel was opened in 1812 by the Hay Tramroad and was afterwards taken over by the B&MR and enlarged by Henry Conybeare. Reopened by the B&MR on 1 May 1863 it was claimed to be the oldest railway tunnel in the country. *Courtesy P. Korrison*

Right: The former Mid Wales Railway boundary marker post. The MWR was absorbed by the Cambrian Railways in 1904, but the boundary post survived on the loop at Talyllyn right up to the final closure. *Courtesy C. C. Green*

third class and a first/second composite in the centre of the rake.

The normal service between Brecon and Newport was of three trains a day; the Rhymney branch had seven trains a day with extras on Saturdays: the Merthyr and Dowlais branches had six round trips a day. The South Wales-Aberystwyth summer trains were worked over the East Loop at Talyllyn. The Cambrian Railways provided most of the through coaches from Cardiff, the TVR and Rhymney Railway and Newport. For some years Cambrian 4-4-0s and 0-6-0s worked through to Merthyr returning the next day on the up train. Alternatively, Taff Vale 'M' class 0-6-2Ts worked through to Talyllyn and changed engines there with the Cambrian. These varied workings were instituted to assist the B&MR through the years when it was short of locomotives.

The earliest returns available for 1868 give a total of 528 wagons owned. These were typical of the time — mostly dumb-buffered and of six tons capacity. Through the years there was considerable rebuilding and renewing in Machen Shops — over 300 wagons were rebuilt as fixed-sided rail and ore wagons. After the closure of the

Above: Brecon Free Street station with a Cambrian Railways Mid Wales line train in the bay line; a Midland Railway Swansea-Hereford train in the up platform; and in the down platform a B&MR Newport-Brecon train. A peculiarity of Brecon station was that there was no footbridge at anytime. *Courtesy T. Watkins*

Below: The B&MR staff at Brecon after World War 1, the coaches in the rear are Cambrian. Today this might seem a very large staff but in the days when the railway was the usual means of travel the staff was hard pressed at times. *Courtesy M. E. MortonLloyd*

Rhymney Ironworks in 1891 these wagons were replaced by open wagons of a more modern pattern. The impending withdrawal of all dumb buffered wagons from 31 December 1913 forced Machen to fit Turton self-contained buffers to its later renewals. Much of the oldest wagon stock was replaced by steel-framed wagons supplied by various makers on hire purchase terms. After the grouping many of these wagons were fitted with oil axleboxes and other GWR fittings. The last survivors were withdrawn as late as 1956.

The goods workings of the B&MR were in two distinct patterns on the Rhymney branch and the Northern Section. The Rhymney branch's easy gradients favoured loaded trains heading down to the docks. Originally traffic came from the Rhymney Ironworks; luckily when local iron ore was exhausted and the Ironworks' operations became uneconomic, the sinking of additional collieries gave the B&MR an even more lucrative traffic. Eventually the Barry and GW were working two trips each a day besides the six that the B&MR worked themselves — in addition to six colliers trains a day that the B&MR provided locomotives for, the collieries providing the coaches.

The traffic in the Northern district, with its heavy gradients was mostly agricultural, timber, road stone etc. There was also quite substantial traffic from Merthyr and Dowlais for northern destinations. This was handed over to the Cambrian and Midland Railways at Talyllyn Junction — Talyllyn being a major interchange point with a staff of 80 in 1914. World War 1 saw a reversal

of the mode of working, as coal exports through the docks dwindled. The best steam coal was now reserved for the Royal Navy, and as the GWR and LNWR joint Shrewsbury-Hereford line could not cope with the sheer volume of 'Jellicoe Specials' heading north for Invergordon and Scapa Flow, the B&MR was called upon to work up to four of these trains a day up to Talyllyn Junction, there they were handed over to the Cambrian, which worked them over the Mid Wales Railway and ultimately passed them on to the Great Central Railway at Wrexham. Double-headed and with two bank engines in the rear, the B&MR trains blasted their way up to Torpantau — with many of their staff in the armed forces, and others working the military railways in France, the B&MR rose to the occasion; some of their old servants say that the last cinders from these trains have not landed yet!

Most of the original station buildings were of a temporary nature, built of timber with clap-boarded exteriors. By 1896 only Dolygaer and Dowlais Top had not been replaced. The best of the replacement buildings — as at Rhiwderin and Talybont-on-Usk — were constructed of dressed stone and were of a solid and pleasing appearance.

Most of the original signalboxes and equipment was supplied by Duttons of Worcester and after that firm was taken over by McKenzie Holland; somersault signals were the order of the day. The single line sections were originally worked by Staff and Ticket, but in 1892 Tyers No 5 Tablet Instruments were introduced while the double line sections were controlled by Tyers one-wire two-position block instruments.

This highly individualistic little railway, with its marvellous 'esprit de corps', was like a large family and its staff, having learned their trade on its fearsome gradients, was much sought after by other railways. It came to the end of its independent existence on 24 July 1922 when it was absorbed by its old opponent the GWR.

The Burry Port & Gwendraeth Valley Railway

The origins of the BPGVR go back to 1765 and the construction of Kymer's Canal (which was the first in Wales) and the first link in the chain to improve shipping facilities for the anthracite of the Gwendraeth Valley through the small harbour of Kidwelly. This was superseded by the Kidwelly & Llanelly Canal & Tramroad of 1812, incorporated to improve the harbour of Kidwelly and build tramroads and railways instead of canals. This was followed by the Pembrey Harbour Company of 1825 empowered to build a harbour at Pembrey and construct a canal, railway or tramroad to connect it to the rest of the canal system. This last development was necessary because of insurmountable problems with regard to the silting up of the Gwendraeth Estuary at Kidwelly. The Harbour Company changed its name to the Burry Port Company in 1835 and the new harbour became known as Burry Port. The canal company changed its title yet again in 1866 to the Kidwelly & Burry Port Railway Company. The following year this was dissolved and control of its undertakings vested in the railway company as the Burry Port & Gwendraeth Valley Railway Company. The conversion of the canal to a railway commenced and was completed up to Cymmawr by 1869. Most authorities state that the railway was built on the bed of the canal; this is only partially correct — the former towpath was used as track formation except at existing bridges and aqueducts. This gave the BPGVR the very restricted gauge clearances that were always a problem.

The conversion of the Kidwelly branch

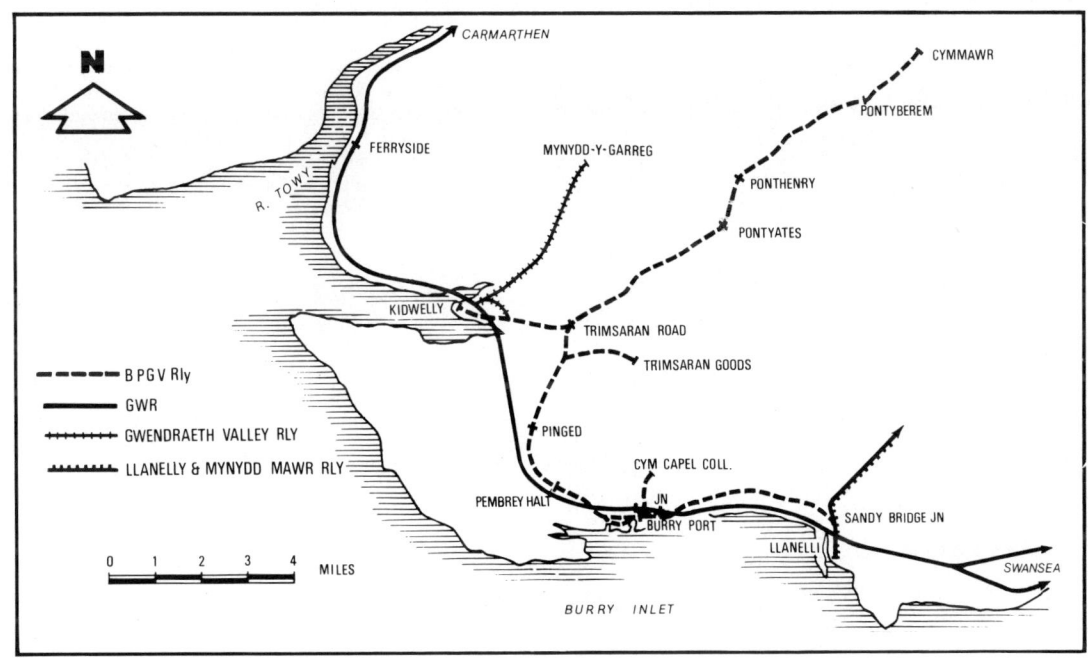

Above left: *Mountaineer* just before withdrawal in 1891 when it was described as 'worn out'. However the boiler shell was used in the construction of a culvert in the docks and the bogies were used as trolley wagons for a number of years. *Courtesy J. W. Evans*

Above: The second Fairlie, a much larger machine, was an 0-6-0+0-6-0 built by Cross & Co of St Helens. It was one of a batch of three built for the 3ft 6in gauge Queensland Railway. It was returned to this country as unsuitable and after regauging by the Yorkshire Engine Co arrived at Burry Port in 1878. Named *Victoria* it is pictured at Pontyates in 1897 after reboilering the previous year. *Courtesy G. Davies*

Left: Pontyberem station on opening day. This was to be the terminus for passenger trains until 1913 when services were extended to Cymmawr. The station is not quite complete — the signal spectacle plates have not had glasses fitted. The track is of the newly laid 75lb per yard 'improved' flat-bottomed pattern.
Courtesy B. Cripps

Below left: In 1909 the first of a new class of locomotive arrived; they were to satisfy the BPGVR to the end of its days. Hudswell Clarke 0-6-0T No 8 *Pioneer* arrived in an experimental livery of crimson lake instead of the usual light green, but the lining of black and white was the same; it is here seen at Burry Port just after entering service. *Courtesy of G. Davies*

followed in 1873; the final branch to Sandy Gate, Llanelly on the alignment of an old tramroad was opened in 1891 this linked the BPGVR with the Llanelly & Mynydd Mawr Railway.

For most of this period the BPGVR was in the hands of a receiver because of the excessive costs of the conversion, coupled with the failure of the Pontyberem Colliery Company and a general decline in demand for Gwendraeth anthracite. However, during the 1890s trade began to expand and the BPGVR managed to discharge the receiver in 1898, by economic methods of working and a policy of making and maintaining its equipment by its own staff. The BPGVR was paying a dividend of 10% within 10 years and it maintained this percentage for the rest of its existence.

In 1898 the BPGVR was approached by the colliery companies to run workmen's trains. Because of the recent insolvency and the reluctance of the BPGVR to embark on additional expenditure, the following compromise was adopted. Each colliery bought coaches with accommodation for 100 men and paid the BPGVR £2 10s 0d per coach per week used. The colliery companies recovered their outlay by deducting one shilling per week from the wages of the men using the trains. Soon colliers' wives began using the trains on market days. The BPGVR allowed them to travel free but charged them sixpence on every shopping basket and package carried.

Another local practice was that in the summer, on Bank Holidays and Mabon's Days, trains of coal wagons were swept out, benches placed in them and everyone had a free trip to Burry Port to spend a day by the sea.

Unfortunately, in August 1903 there was a collision between a light engine and a workmen's train. An investigation of this event by the Board of Trade revealed that some of the passengers on the train were not colliers. The presence of the manager of the BPGVR was requested in London for an interview with Col H. A. York (head of the Railway Inspectorate) to explain the irregular practices of the BPGVR and there the former received the formal censure and displeasure of the Board of Trade for allowing such practices.

The directors of the BPGVR decided, therefore, to convert their main line to a passenger line under the provisions of the Light Railway Acts. In the meantime the practice of allowing the market day passengers to travel on the colliers' trains was to continue despite the risks incurred by defying the Board of Trade.

H. F. Stephens (afterwards Colonel) was engaged as consultant engineer to supervise the realignment of curves and gradients and the general renewal of rolling stock and equipment to prepare the BPGVR for its new role. The main line from Burry Port to Pontyberem was passed by the Board of Trade on 2 August 1909. The remaining two miles to Cymmawr had to be completely realigned and did not open for passenger trains till 1913.

The first engines to work on the BPGVR were

Left: Little No 3 at Burry Port; a Chapman & Furneaux product No 3 was almost identical to the small Peckett tanks that the BPGVR used for shunting and working trips to the collieries. Note directly behind the stopblocks, the conveniently situated Neptune Hotel — still surviving to this day, unfortunately this example of Victorian domestic architecture has been disfigured by modern development.
Courtesy G. Davies

the contractor's engines *Lizzie* and *Gwendraeth*, both small 0-4-0STs built by Hughes of Loughborough. *Gwendraeth* was taken over by the BPGVR and survived till 1906 working as a shunter in the dock.

For working the coal trains the BPGVR was persuaded to invest in a pair of Fairlie's Patent engines. The first was obtained in 1870 — an 0-4-0+0-4-0T originally intended for the Swedish Oscarham Railway. Named *Mountaineer* by the BPGVR, the engine was withdrawn in 1891. The bogies were used as boiler trucks, and the boiler shells were used as linings to a culvert in the dock.

The second Fairlie was a much larger engine than *Mountaineer*. Named *Victoria* the engine was an 0-6-0+0-6-0T built for the 3ft 6in gauge Queensland State Railway. Returned by that railway as unacceptable, *Victoria* was regauged by the Yorkshire Engine Co and arrived at Burry Port in 1873. It was reboilered in 1896 and finally withdrawn in 1903.

Right, top to bottom: No 9 a slightly larger version of *Pioneer* at Burry Port. The second wagon on this goods train is a former Midland Railway van — with the exception of locomotives, the BPGVR believed in shopping around on the secondhand market for the rest of its rolling stock. *Courtesy G. Davies*

At the time of the grouping, No 8 *Pioneer* was in the workshops for a general repair. Because of postwar shortages and the upheaval of grouping it did not return to traffic till April 1924. Seen here with John Eager and his workshop staff, *Pioneer* was to be the last locomotive to be turned out from Burry Port after a general repair from then on. With the exception of boiler repairs, the BPGVR tackled everything else. After this the workshop's staff and machinery were dispersed and, in fact, after a few more years the dock itself was abandoned. *Courtesy G. Davies*

With some of its postwar repatriation money, the BPGVR bought two new goods brake vans. Built by Hurst Nelson, of Great Central Railway design, they were probably the only new items of rolling stock the BPGVR ever possessed. *Courtesy HMRS*

The terminus station at Burry Port looking up the line from the stop blocks. The station buildings clad in corrugated iron became almost a trade mark of Col H. F. Stephens on his various light railways. *Courtesy R. E. Bowen*

In 1876 the BPGVR began working the neighbouring Gwendraeth Valley Railway and acquired its little Fox Walker 0-6-0ST *Kidwelly*, which gave good service until it was sold in 1903.

With only four engines available, the locomotive position was precarious to say the least, but the financial position did not permit any expenditure on additional stock. However, in 1886 a second-hand Manning Wardle 0-6-0ST was purchased; named *Burry Port* by the BPGVR it was eventually sold in 1901.

By 1890 with both the Fairlie engines in desperate need of heavy repairs if they were to continue in service, the improving financial state of the BPGVR enabled the company to acquire a new Peckett 0-6-0ST. Named *Dyvatty* it arrived in 1891 but unfortunately developed serious boiler defects within two years. Always a problem engine, it was sold in 1906. A far better purchase was another Manning Wardle 0-6-0ST from the Ynyscedwyn Colliery; in BPGVR service the engine was named *Cwm Mawr*.

By the end of the century the BPGVR's finances had improved enough for the Receiver to be discharged and the company to renew completely its entire locomotive stock. Between 1900 and 1907 seven 0-6-0STs were bought, five by the Avonside Engine Co and two similar by Chapman & Furneaux. All existing locomotives were sold for scrap or part exchanged for the new arrivals.

For the start of the passenger services in 1909, a Hudswell Clarke 0-6-0T was ordered. This locomotive was numbered 8 and named *Pioneer*. It was an instant success, thanks to its larger

boiler and firebox coupled with a short wheelbase, and eight more of slightly larger dimensions were acquired. Nameless, as from now on BPGVR engines were only numbered, they took over all the main line workings, the saddle tanks being relegated to dock shunting and trip working. After the grouping most of the BPGVR engines stayed in the locality with the exception of two of the 0-6-0STs — *Kidwelly* and *Cym Mawr* — which were tranferred to Weymouth Quay in 1926. To supplement the BPGVR engines the GWR transferred in its standard 0-6-0Ts of the '19xx' and '20xx' series. I wonder what BPGVR enginemen thought when they had to shunt the exposed Glynhebog Colliery sidings with an open-backed cab engine in the teeth of a westerly gale blowing straight off the Irish Sea!

In 1908, to work the new passenger services, the BPGVR purchased 10 Metropolitan eight-wheeled coaches. These were not bogie coaches; the inner pair of wheels were fixed and the outer pair were mounted in a radial truck giving a certain amount of flexibility through the swing links. Some of these coaches were classified as workmen's, replacing the colliery-owned coaches on the colliers' trains. Additional coaches were obtained in 1910 when three LSWR four-wheelers were purchased. Most authorities say that these coaches were originally six-wheeled and had the middle pair removed before service on the BPGVR. However, LSWR records clearly indicate that they were always four-wheeled. Two years later another three LSWR coaches and a Metropolitan brake third were added to stock.

For the opening to Cymmawr, a further eight

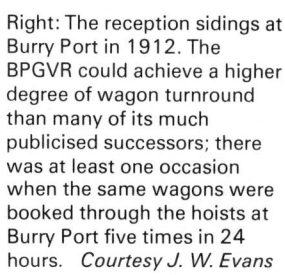

Right: The reception sidings at Burry Port in 1912. The BPGVR could achieve a higher degree of wagon turnround than many of its much publicised successors; there was at least one occasion when the same wagons were booked through the hoists at Burry Port five times in 24 hours. *Courtesy J. W. Evans*

Right: The first wagon being tipped through the first of two hydraulic wagon hoists brought into use at Burry Port on 18 June 1904. These were designed by John Eager (who besides being the locomotive, carriage and wagon engineer had charge as well of the dock machinery) and built by the BPGVR itself.
Courtesy G. Davies

Centre right: The yard staff at Burry Port in 1914 — some of the men who, for comparatively little money, would work long hours so that Gwendraeth anthracite could be despatched promptly. *Courtesy R. E. Bowen*

Bottom right: The dock at Burry Port pre-1900 when it occupied an area of 64,000sq ft with a total quayage of 504ft. This was barely adequate in its heyday when, on normal tides, vessels of 2,000 tons burden could be accommodated. Besides the hydraulic hoists and capstans it was lit by electric light from the BPGVR's own powerhouse. Whilst there was considerable cross-channel trade with North Devon and Cornwall, a respectable amount of anthracite was despatched to Brittany and northern Spain with lead and copper ore as a return cargo. *Courtesy G. Davies*

Metropolitan eight-wheeled coaches arrived at Burry Port. Finally in 1920 five North London Railway four-wheeled coaches completed the BPGVR's requirements. This mixed collection of coaches fitted with vacuum brakes and lit by acetylene gas sufficed for the third class only service of three or four trains a day either way, with an additional two on Saturdays. After the grouping the GWR drafted in low-roofed four-wheeled coaches of their own and withdrew the BPGVR coaches very rapidly. In the 1930s the GWR built some modern steel-panelled bogie coaches with a low roof profile as their own stock of suitable four-wheeled stock was diminishing. But on the last day of passenger services on the former BPGVR four-wheeled coaches were still in use.

The goods stock of the BPGVR likewise was almost entirely second-hand. At the grouping they handed over eight open wagons, eight vans and nine goods brake vans. Two of the goods brake vans were of Great Central design and were almost new, having been purchased with Government Repatriation Funds in 1920. The origin of most of the remainder is unknown and they were condemned by the GWR almost straight away.

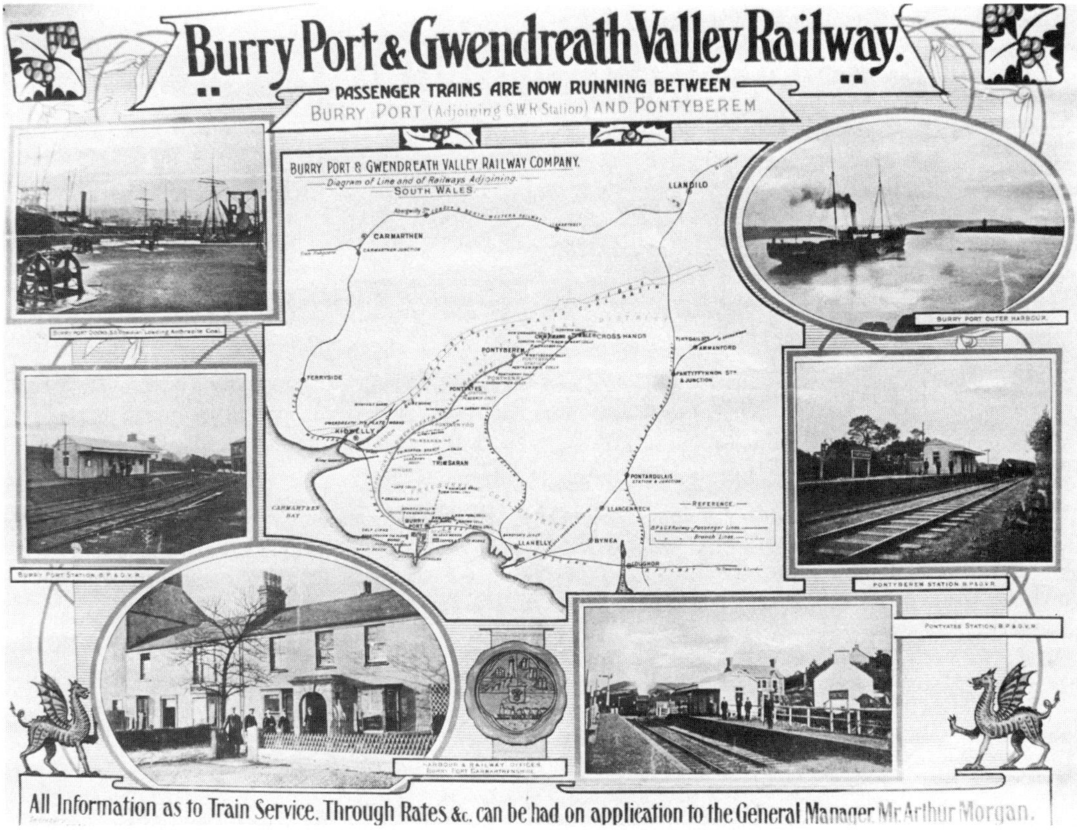

Above: For a small railway, the BPGVR was very publicity minded. In December 1909 it produced this card which contains a spelling error in its heading title.
Courtesy J. W. Evans

Below: This bridge restriction plate from an overbridge at Burry Port is however correctly spelt.
Courtesy J. W. Evans

Below: A BPGVR cash box that still survives in private ownership — curiously with the same incorrect spelling.   *Courtesy J. W. Evans*

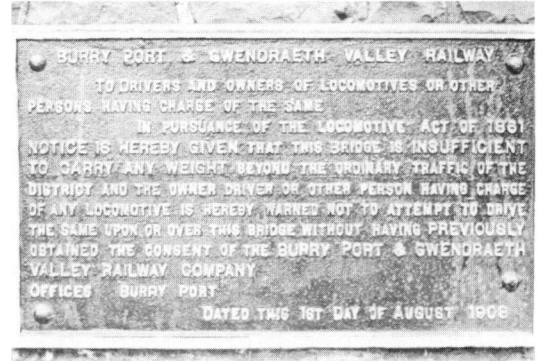

The station buildings were timber-framed, corrugated iron sheeted structures that were almost a standard fitting on a Col Stephens railway. Little corrugated iron huts were provided on the sleeper and earth platforms of the halts.

The main line trains were controlled by the electric train staff, the signalboxes and signals were supplied by the Railway Signal Co. No distants were ever installed on the BPGVR. The main line was relaid entirely with an 'improved' flat bottom rail of 75lb to the yard.

The corrugated iron locomotive sheds and adjoining workshops at Burry Port were kept very busy. The company did all its own locomotive repairs there except for heavy boiler repairs, and as well as carrying out urgent repairs for collieries and maintaining all the dock machinery, there was little that the BPGVR could not do. Under the GWR the workshops were closed, the staff and machinery dispersed and, unfortunately, within a few years the dock itself was closed and abandoned.

The last locomotive to have a heavy repair at Burry Port was old No 8 *Pioneer*, which emerged in BPGVR livery with the addition of GWR numberplates in 1924. *Pioneer* was seen working on the former Cleobury Mortimer & Ditton Priors Light Railway in 1932, with BPGVR light green just discernible beneath a generous coat of GWR grime.

The BPGVR was absorbed by the GWR on 24 July 1922.

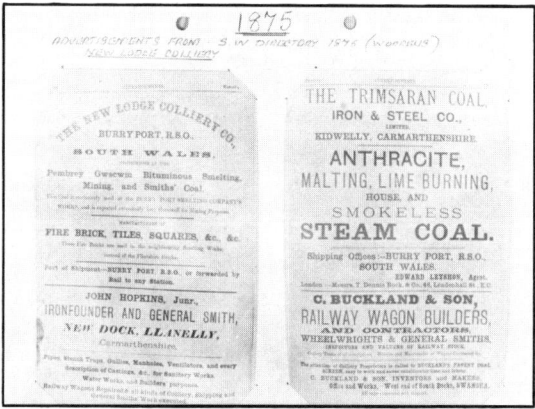

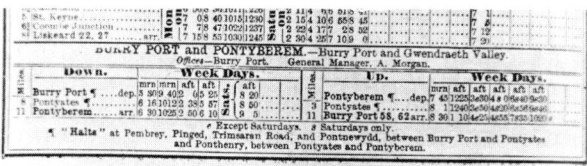

Right, top to bottom: On the realigned railway between Ponty berem and Cymmawr a new type of warning notice without any title at all was used on the ungated level crossings. *Courtesy J. W. Evans*

Two advertisements by Gwendraeth Valley collieries that were inserted in the 1875 edition of *Worrell's South Wales Directory*. *Courtesy G. Davies*

The August 1909 edition of *Bradshaw's Railway Timetable* contained the first entry for a passenger service on the BPGVR — respectability at last! *Courtesy J. W. Evans*

A post-grouping scene at Burry Port. The GWR quickly scrapped the existing coaches, bringing in various four-wheeled coaches of their own manufacture. Some of these lasted as long as the passenger service; in fact on the last day in 1953 it was still possible to ride in a four-wheeled coach. *Courtesy T. Watkins*

The Cardiff Railway

In 1830 the second Marquis of Bute obtained an Act of Parliament for the construction of the Bute Ship Canal & Dock near the small town of Cardiff, so that he could expedite the development of his extensive mineral concessions. The first dock, afterwards known as the Bute West Dock, was opened in 1839. The Taff Vale Railway leased facilities there in 1840 and put the dock in direct communication with the collieries of the Rhondda and Taff valleys. The sudden death of the Marquis of Bute, on 18 March 1848, led to the docks and his other extensive interests being placed in the hands of trustees as his heir was under age. They started further extensions: the first portion of the Bute East Dock was brought into use in 1855; and, connected to the Rhymney Railway, in 1857, the East Dock was completed in 1859. The continual pressure of the coal owners to have more facilities to expedite the shipment of Welsh steam coal led to the construction of the Roath Basin in 1874. But the tremendous increase in shipment traffic led to even more congestion, and so the large Roath Dock was undertaken and finally opened in 1887. The Bute Estates levied additional tolls of a penny per ton on all coal shipments to help fund the constructional costs of this dock and this led to problems with a large section of the Rhondda coal owners, who decided to promote the Barry Railway.

The Bute Trustees converted their dock interests into the Bute Dock Company by an act

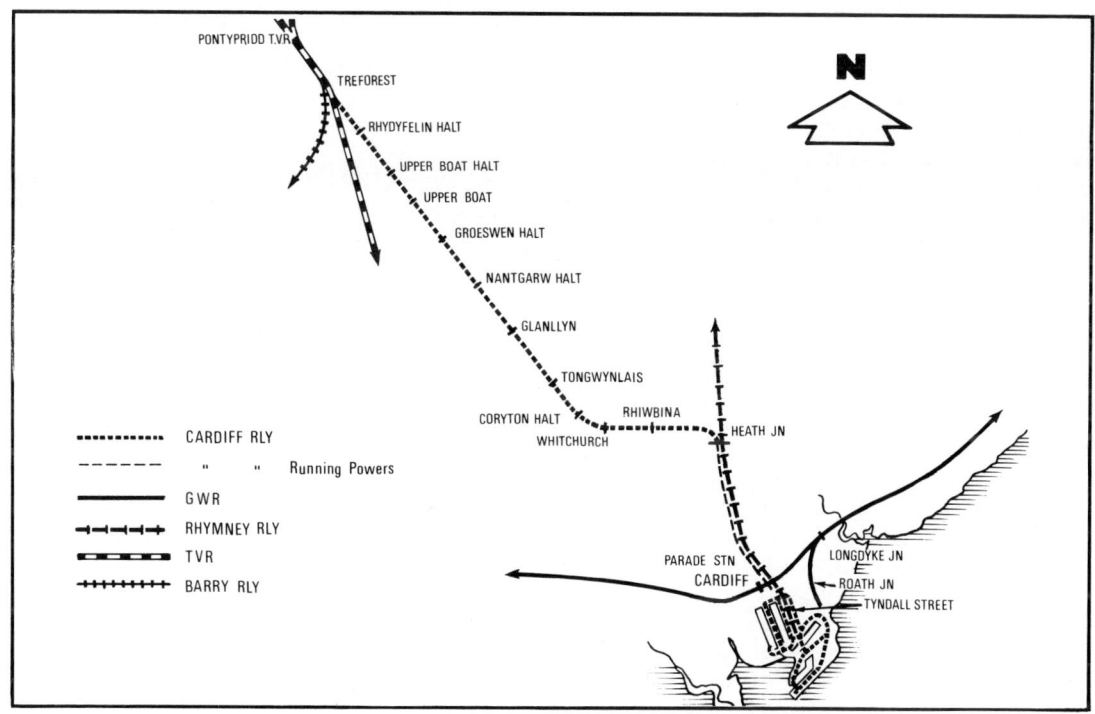

Right: The Cardiff Railway purchased various small engines for dock shunting and trip working around the Bute Estates from several sources, mostly secondhand. The most numerous was a class of 13 0-6-0STs built by the Cardiff engineering firm of Parfitt & Jenkins between 1869 and 1881. After many years of hard work, four were still going strong at grouping, but the GWR had withdrawn them all by 1926. Former Cardiff Railway No 19, now GWR No 697, is seen still at work in the East Dock in 1924. *WRRC*

of June 1886 with the third Marquis of Bute as Chairman. At what period locomotives first worked in the Bute Docks is unknown; it is probable that engines of the TVR performed all duties in the earlier days. The first engines owned by the Bute Estates appeared on the scene when the East Dock was opened. A total of 26 engines was handed over to the Bute Dock Co in 1886.

In an attempt to emulate the success of the Barry Railway in having docks and railway under one management, the Bute Dock Co became the Cardiff Railway by an act granted on 6 August 1897. All its attempts to promote various railways were opposed and defeated except for a line which ran from Treforest on the Taff Vale Railway crossed over the Glamorgan Canal to connect with the Rhymney Railway at the Heath Junction three miles north of Cardiff, and then by means of running powers reached its own dock railway. This railway opened on 15 May 1909, and one special train, hauled by a Cardiff Railway locomotive with the Marquis of Bute on the footplate ran from the Bute Merthyr Collieries at Treherbert and was passed over a temporary junction at Treforest and continued down the Cardiff Railway. Unfortunately the Cardiff Railway's Act only authorised a junction with the passenger lines of the TVR at Treforest. All attempts to remove this impediment were successfully defeated by the TVR on the grounds that the geographical limitations plus the junctions with the Barry Railway and the volume of its own traffic at this point made additional junctions impossible.

The largest extention of the docks was opened

on 13 July 1907 by King Edward VII and named the Queen Alexandra Dock.

With a main line that was restricted to a few local goods trains, the Cardiff Railway, introduced a railmotor service from Rhydyfelin Halt just south of the Treforest river bridge running to the Parade station of the Rhymney Railway. Here a third platform was brought into use for this service which commenced on 1 March 1911. The company had raised £800,000 in debenture shares in 1897 to help finance construction of the new main line, but, denied the coal traffic it was built for, it was necessary to bolster receipts as soon as possible. The debenture shares bearing interest at 4% depressed the returns of the ordinary share holders to 3% in 1910, 2% in 1911, 1% in 1913 and nil in 1914.

In 1909/10 the TVR promoted a bill to absorb the Cardiff and Rhymney Railways. The TVR proposed to purchase the Cardiff Railway for £5,583,000 but the bill was defeated, principally by the opposition of the Barry Railway and Newport shipping interests, and also because the governments of the time were apprehensive of creating monopolies.

In 1917 the premature retirement of the General Manager, C. S. Dennis, led to the Rhymney Railway General Manager, A. E. Prosser, taking on the additional duties at the helm of the Cardiff Railway. This temporary arrangement was to continue for the rest of the uneasy years up to the grouping.

The Cardiff Railway inherited a mixed collection of tank engines from the Bute Dock Co,

Right: A peculiar engine purchased in 1882 was long-boilered pannier tank No 2, with short wheelbase and rear overhang. It is seen here at East Moors in its green livery soon after arrival. The ducal coronet on the side tank was the only clue to its ownership. *Courtesy National Museum Wales*

Left: Another oddity owned by the Cardiff Railway — 0-6-0ST No 24 of uncertain origin was transferred to the docks in 1885 from the Bute colliery at Hirwain. After rebuilding in Tyndall Street Works the former 0-4-2T emerged as an 0-6-0ST. Subsequently it was re-boilered and fitted with an open back cab similar to the Parfitt & Jenkins locomotives. It was never renumbered by the GWR and was withdrawn in May 1922. *WRRC*

Below left: The newly created Cardiff Railway ordered replacement engines with a view to the future main line workings from Treforest. Kitson's supplied two 0-6-2Ts in 1898, one of which, No 10, is seen here performing the humbler shunting duties to which they were reduced to. As GWR No 158, No 10 managed to survive till 1932. *WRRC*

Below: In 1919 the Cardiff Railway took delivery of an additional engine from Kitson's. An 0-6-0T it was similar to others that had been supplied back in 1889 with one difference: the new engine, No 7, was fitted with the vacuum brake so that it could assist on passenger trains as required. It is seen in 1920 at Upper Boat station in smart LNWR style livery attached to a trailer coach set, the usual Cardiff Railway train. *C. H. W. Clifford courtesy C. C. Green*

some had been transfered from collieries owned by the Bute Estates. Many of them had been replaced by more modern engines, more in keeping with its status as a railway company.

The oldest engines handed over to the GWR were four 0-6-0STs built by the Cardiff engineering firm of Parfitt and Jenkins. Originally a class of 13 engines built between 1869 and 1881, they undertook most of the shunting duties in the docks. Their distinctive open backed cabs with square spectacle looks outs in the front plates gave them an almost oriental appearance. They did not last long after the grouping, the last pair being withdrawn in 1926.

Another oddity was No 2 built by Kitson & Co in 1882. An 0-6-0 pannier tank of the old Stephenson long-boilered design No 2 had a wheelbase of only 10ft 9in and spent its life waddling around the docks till 1924.

No 24 was transferred from the Hirwain Colliery in 1883 as a 2-4-2ST and was rebuilt as an 0-6-0ST in Tyndall Street Workshops in 1885. On being reboilered in 1891 No 24 was fitted with a cab similar to the Parfitt & Jenkins engines. The locomotive was withdrawn by the Cardiff Railway in 1922 but was cut up at Swindon later the same year.

The Bute Dock Co, purchased its first 0-6-2T from Kitsons in 1886. Numbered 26 it was the first modern engine with an enclosed cab; it was also fitted with a stove pipe chimney which was retained till repaired at Swindon after the grouping.

The Bute Dock Co ordered five more 0-6-2Ts between 1887 and 1898 with larger fireboxes and higher boiler pressures than No 26. Fitted with Parallel chimneys, two of them were sold to colliery companies in 1931, the remaining pair were withdrawn the next year.

Kitsons also supplied two 0-6-0Ts with a wheelbase of only 13ft 0in; they were very useful in restricted sidings. Another pair arrived in 1899; these had low sloping tops to the side tanks to improve visibility and a cut away in the side tanks to give access to the motion — small boys used to ask the crews from a safe distance 'Is that where you put the key in to wind it up?' Finally, in 1919, No 7 arrived, a modernised version fitted with a vacuum brake becoming the leading passenger engine.

As replacements for the worn out Manning

Wardle tank engines, Kitson's designed two 0-4-0STs fitted with J. Hawthorn-Kitson patent valve gear. Coupled to a wheel base of only 6ft 0in, this was less than that of the wagons that they were usually to be found shunting into very restricted corners. One was scrapped in 1934 the other transferred to Bridgwater Dock in 1943 and was withdrawn from Swansea in 1963. Purchased for preservation, old No 5 is the only Cardiff Railway locomotive still in existence.

Two more 0-6-2Ts arrived from Kitsons in 1905 ready for the opening of the new main line. With extended side tanks with sloping tops, larger coal bunkers and extended smokeboxes, a further pair arrived in 1919. They did not find much favour with the GWR — the last one, withdrawn in 1936, one had a brief life of 11 years.

Like the ADR and the B&MR, the Cardiff Railway was persuaded to invest in three GWR '1661' class 0-6-0STs available at an extremely cheap price after the GWR had failed to sell the entire class 'en bloc'.

48

Left: As happened elsewhere, the railcars developed more traffic than they could manage. In 1914 the Cardiff Railway purchased from the LNWR one of that company's 2-4-2Ts, fitted with nameplates *The Earl of the Dumfries* (a hereditary title of the Bute family). This engine took over the passenger trains with the trailer coaches, and when the railmotors were converted into additional trailer cars they were pressed back into service. At grouping the GWR withdrew the ex-LNWR engine immediately.　*WRRC*

Below left: In an attempt to develop alternative traffic over the main line that the TVR had thwarted so successfully, the Cardiff Railway commenced a railmotor service on 1 March 1911. The similarity to contemporary GWR railmotors can be seen in this photograph of the inaugural trip at Whitchurch with directors and officials. *Courtesy C. W. Harris*

Above right: In addition to the two railmotors, two additional trailer cars were ordered from the makers, the Gloucester Carriage & Wagon Co. Here trailer No 4 emerges from that company's workshops in 1911: with the dark red lower panels and white upper works, the similarity to the LNWR livery was marked.　*WRRC*

Right: The upper limit of passenger workings was Rhyd-Y-Felin. It had a rail level halt and a fenced in circulating area in front, the gate to which was kept locked. Intending passengers were let out by the railmotor guard. The Cardiff Railway also adopted the somersault signal in line with the majority of Welsh railways.　*Courtesy B. Stevens*

Below: The impressive bridge over the River Taff between Rhyd-y-Felin and Treforest was rarely used apart from its initial testing and the inaugural coal train. It was certainly surplus to requirements at grouping, but nevertheless survived intact until demolished for scrap during the last war.　*Courtesy C. W. Harris*

Right: In 1927 former Cardiff Railway No 29 was sold out of service by the GWR as No 692 to the Ebbw Vale Steel, Iron & Coal Co. Fitted with nameplates the engine became No 38 *Irthlingborough* and is seen here under new ownership in 1936. It was finally withdrawn at Scunthorpe in 1957. *Courtesy WRRC*

Also for main line working Kitson's supplied three large 0-6-2Ts very similar to the '04' class of the TVR except they had larger coal bunkers and extended side tanks. In 1928 No 35 (as GWR No 155) was rebuilt with a taper boiler. Being the only Cardiff Railway engine to be honoured in this way, it survived to be nationalised before being withdrawn in 1953.

The 1911 railmotor service was operated by two railmotor cars with two additional trailers built by the Gloucester Carriage & Wagon Co which had the engine units built by the nearby engineering firm of Sissons Ltd. In 1920 the railmotors were withdrawn and the bodies rebuilt in a similar manner to the trailers though the driving compartments were also removed. The former railmotors and trailers were then used as coaches attached to one of the vacuum-fitted locomotives.

By 1914 it was accepted that the railmotors could not really manage an additional trailer in times of heavy traffic, so an ex-LNWR 2-4-2T was purchased from Crewe. This entered service fitted with nameplates entitled *Earl of Dumfries* (the hereditary title of the eldest son of the Bute family) and its usual train was the two trailer cars. The LNWR lining was afterwards adopted by the Cardiff Railway for its principal engines.

The last engines obtained were four heavy duty 0-6-0STs for dock shunting. Supplied by Hudswell Clarke, they were rebuilt as pannier tanks by the GWR and carried on working at Cardiff until withdrawn between 1953 and 1955.

The coaching stock at grouping consisted of the four ex-railmotor cars and trailers, plus four ex-Hull & Barnsley Railway four-wheeled coaches purchased in 1919 to form a workmen's train. These were soon withdrawn by the GWR, while the former rail motors and trailers were fitted with the GWR form of auto-train gear and entered service as trailers. Being very similar to GWR auto-train trailers when they were built, they were now only distinguishable by minor details.

The wagon stock at the end consisted of 30 open wagons, 10 vans and three goods brake vans, while another 700 open wagons were on hire at the time. This last fact illustrates the lack of revenue from the relatively expensive main line — no money has been available to buy rolling stock.

The Cardiff Railway commenced its passenger services with 11 trains a day with five on Sundays. In 1931 the GWR cut the service back to Coryton Halt and virtually abandoned the rest of the former main line. A brisk service of 20 trains a day was run over the rest of the system.

Like most of its neighbours, the Cardiff's signals were the somersault type as supplied by McKenzie & Holland and the block instruments were the Tyers two-position one-wire pattern.

The final dividend of the Cardiff Railway was $1\frac{1}{2}$% on the ordinary shares in 1921. The mileage returns give an insight into the lack of traffic on the abortive main line: passenger train miles 66,000, dock and shunting mileage 446,000, main line goods trains 10,000 miles. Grouping overtook the Cardiff Railway on 25 March 1922 when it became the smallest constituent company of the GWR group.

The LNWR in Wales

The LNWR lines in South Wales had a common base, the Shrewsbury & Hereford Railway. Incorporated on 3 August 1846 the Shrewsbury & Hereford opened throughout in 1853, and was worked under a nine-year lease by Thomas Brassey, the contractor who constructed it. From 1 July 1862 the S&HR was jointly leased by the GWR, LNWR and West Midland Railway. The first link in the chain was the promotion of the Knighton Railway — incorporated by an Act of Parliament dated 21 May 1858 — to build a line from a junction on the Shrewsbury & Hereford Railway near an inn called the 'Craven Arms' through the valleys of the Onny, Teme and Clun to Knighton. The first portion to Bucknell was opened on 1 October 1860, built and worked by the same Thomas Brassey. The remaining section to Knighton was opened on 6 March 1861. An agreement to co-operate with the LNWR was entered into on 1 May 1861; this was followed by the LNWR taking over the working of the Knighton Railway on 1 July 1862.

The LNWR had been actively supporting a Central Wales Railway which proposed to build a railway from Knighton to Llandrindod Wells. A conflicting proposal from the Oswestry & Newtown and its associated companies was the construction of a railway from Moat Lane through Llanidloes, Builth Wells to Llandovery. The LNWR and its adherents were overjoyed when the Central Wales Railway Act was granted on 13 August 1859 while their opponents' bill was only authorised to Llanidloes. The first two miles of the Central Wales Railway to Knucklas was opened in 1862. An Act of Almalgamation with the Knighton Railway was obtained on 21 May 1863. A further act, known as the Central Wales Railways Act, was obtained on 22 June 1863 and authorised the LNWR to maintain, work and provide locomotives and rolling stock for the amalgamated companies. The remainder of the Central Wales Railway to Llandrindod was opened on 10 October 1865.

Below: The Central Wales line was worked by Webb 2-4-2Ts and 'DX' 0-6-0s during the latter years of the last century. Both classes coped well with the gradients and variable loadings that could all too often be heavy. Here is 'DX' No 1373 blowing off steam at Knighton shed. *G. M. Perkins courtesy C. C. Green*

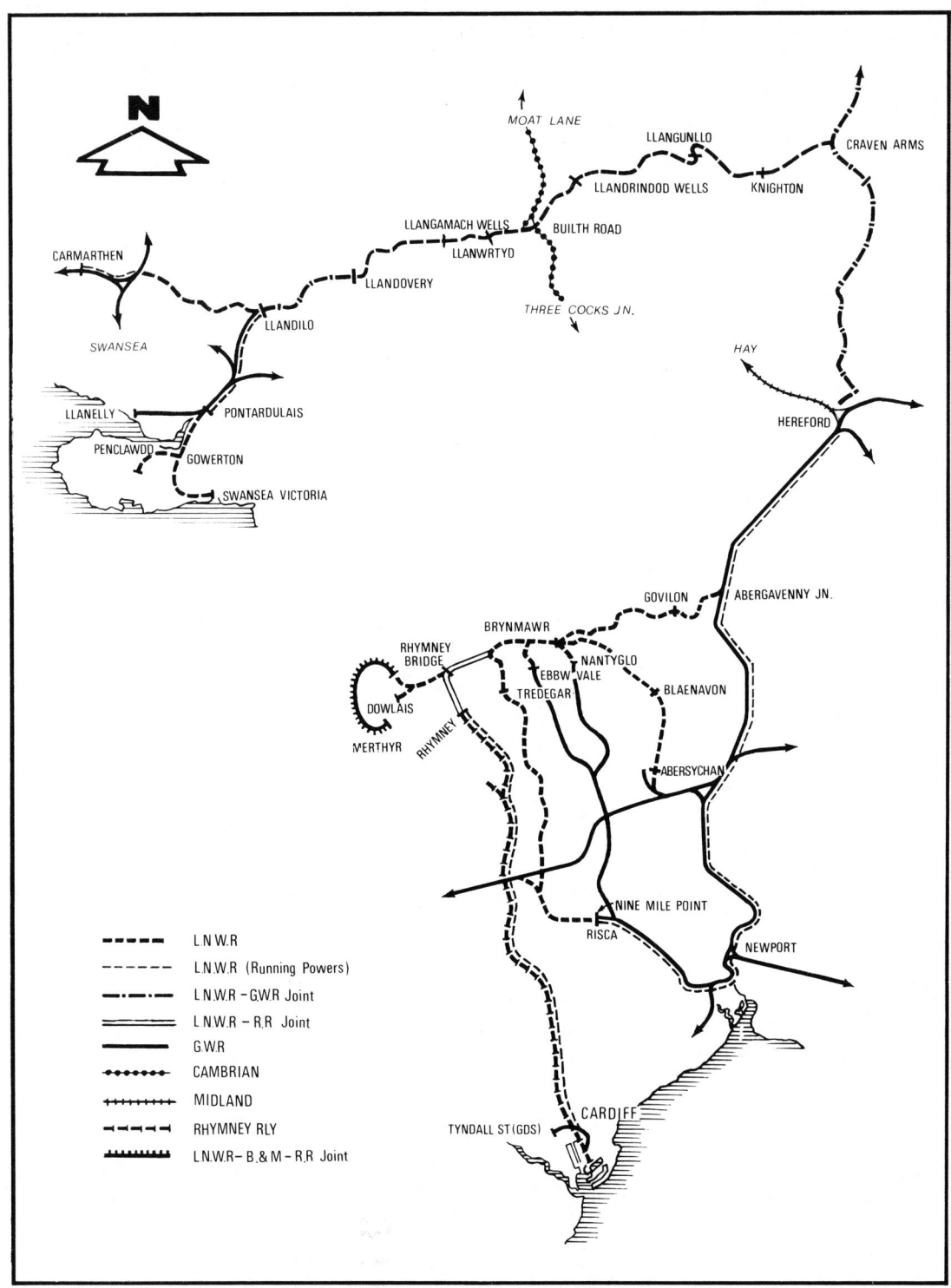

N

MOAT LANE

LLANGUNLLO

CRAVEN ARMS

LLANDRINDOD WELLS   KNIGHTON

LLANGAMACH WELLS   BUILTH ROAD

LLANWRTYD

CARMARTHEN

LLANDOVERY

THREE COCKS JN.

SWANSEA

LLANDILO

HAY

LLANELLY   PONTARDULAIS

HEREFORD

PENCLAWDD

GOWERTON

SWANSEA VICTORIA

GOVILON   ABERGAVENNY JN.

BRYNMAWR

RHYMNEY
BRIDGE   NANTYGLO

EBBW VALE

DOWLAIS   TREDEGAR   BLAENAVON

MERTHYR   RHYMNEY

ABERSYCHAN

NINE MILE POINT

RISCA   NEWPORT

CARDIFF

TYNDALL ST (GDS)

L.N.W.R
L.N.W.R (Running Powers)
L.N.W.R – G.W.R Joint
L.N.W.R – R.R Joint
G.W.R
CAMBRIAN
MIDLAND
RHYMNEY RLY
L.N.W.R – B.& M – R.R Joint

Above: In 1911 Bowen Cooke brought out his superheated 4-6-2T, and some of the class was soon at work on the Central Wales line. Though comparatively small engines for their wheel arrangement, they were a big advance on previous locomotives. Here No 2667 takes water at Knighton in 1912 on a 'Wells Express'.
G. M. Perkins courtesy C. C. Green

Above right: Fowler 2-6-4T No 2385 at Builth Road; with their larger water tanks and ample coal bunker, the 2-6-4Ts were ideal for bank engine workings which they took over when displaced from other duties by the Stanier Class 5s. The last survivors were taken over by the Western Region after nationalisation. *WRRC*

Right: It was a practice of the LNWR to couple displaced locomotives to a combined saloon and coal bunker for the District Engineer to use to get around his district on inspections. For many years the South Wales Engineer was previously *Locomotive* — a former Allan 6ft 0in single built in 1852. This engine was displaced by the famous *Cornwall*.
G. M. Perkins courtesy C. C. Green

A Central Wales Extension Railway was incorporated on 3 July 1860 to build on from Llandrindod Wells to a junction with the Vale of Towy Railway at Llandovery. The CWER was a much more expensive railway to construct and opened to Builth Road on 1 November 1866. Here a connecting loop was made to its former rival, which as the Mid-Wales Railway was finally authorised to build a railway between Llanidloes, Rhayader and connect with the HH&BR at Three Cocks Junction gaining access to Brecon. Further extensions of the CWER enabled the opening to Llanwrtyd Wells on 6 May 1867. The next development stage of the CWER was the climb to the Sugar Loaf Tunnel and then the descent down the valley on a shelf cut in the flanks of Bryn Nichol, culminating in the Cynghordy Viaduct, whose 18 arches spanned the valley of the Bran, before reaching Llandovery. It proved to be impossible to build this section within the time limits of the CWER's original act, so an extension of time act was obtained in 1867 to cover the last 10 miles to Llandovery, which was reached by LNWR trains on 1 June 1868.

The Vale of Towy Railway had been opened between Llandeilo and Llandovery on 1 April 1858, from which date it had been leased for 10 years to the Llanelly Railway. This lease, when it was renewed from 1 April 1868, was jointly held by the Knighton Railway, the Central Wales Railway, The Central Wales Extension Railway, and the Llanelly Railway & Dock Company.

The Llanelly Railway had been incorporated on 19 June 1828 to build a dock at Llanelly and construct a two-mile long horse drawn tramroad to collieries to the north. In 1835 additional powers were obtained to construct a railway up the Loughor Valley to Llandeilo, the first portion to Pontardulais being opened on 1 June 1839. A branch line to Garnant, so that collieries in the Amman Valley could ship anthracite through the dock at Llanelly, was opened on 10 March 1840. This branch line was extended to Brynamman in 1842.

Further extensions towards Llandeilo were opened in 1841 and that town was reached on 24 January 1857. Locomotives were first introduced in 1842. In 1861 the Llanelly Railway, with the assistance of the LNWR, obtained an Act to build a railway from Pontardulais to the South Dock at Swansea. Two branches were also authorised — one from Llandeilo to a junction at Abergwili to reach the broad gauge Carmarthen & Cardigan Railway and lay a third rail on to reach Carmarthen Junction of the South Wales Railway. The second branch line was from Gower Road station to Penclawdd utilising the bed of a canal. The Carmarthen branch opened for goods trains on 14 November 1864; passenger services commenced on 1 June 1865.

The Swansea line opened for goods trains to South Dock Swansea early in 1866. Passenger trains were delayed until 14 December 1867 because of delays in the completion of the Victoria passenger terminus.

The 1868 amended leasing of the Vale of Towy Railway gave the LNWR running powers to Swansea, Llanelly and Carmarthen. The Llanelly Railway, now becoming alarmed at the extent of the LNWR's penetrations tried to repudiate these running powers. A lengthy legal battle ensued but eventually the House of Lords gave a final judgement in favour of the LNWR. In 1871 the LNWR promoted a bill by which the Carmarthen branch and the line from Pontardulais to Swansea became vested in the Swansea & Carmarthen Railway with the LNWR working it. The Swansea line with the Penclawdd branch was purchased by the LNWR in 1872; the Carmarthen branch was finally absorbed in 1892.

The dismembered Llanelly Railway — with its newer and more profitable branches literally torn from its body — now lost heart and concluded an agreement with the GWR and was leased by that company from 1 January 1873.

So the LNWR had finished up owning the Vale of Towy Railway jointly with the GWR and the LNWR also had running powers between Llandeilo and Pontardulais. The company was therefore poised to penetrate further into West Wales towards the 'El Dorado' of Milford Haven, and this would give the GWR some anxious times in the years ahead.

To gain access to the developing industrial activities of South Wales on 8 November 1861 the LNWR leased the Merthyr, Tredegar & Abergavenny Railway while it was still being constructed, much to the dismay of the West Midland Railway which had been preparing a similar bill to lease the MT&AR. Incorporated in

Right: Knucklas station in 1910 had a single platform and single siding goods yard; it stood between Knighton and Llangunllo, just beyond a 13-arch stone viaduct spanning the Teme Valley. In post-grouping years it was reduced to a halt.
G. M. Perkins courtesy C. C. Green

Centre right: Builth Road with its connecting loop to the Cambrian Railways in the centre. When King George V opened the Talgarth Hospital in 1921, the LNWR Royal Train drew on to this loop and the royal party transferred to a Cambrian train on the adjacent siding by means of a specially constructed gangway.
G. M. Perkins courtesy C. C. Green

Below right: The Central Wales Extension Railway obtained an extension of time act in 1867 because of the heavy engineering work encountered. The line bored through the 1,000yd Sugar Loaf Tunnel, descended for four miles at 1 in 60 on a ledge cut into the flank of Bryn Nichol and curved around the Cynghordy Viaduct. This viaduct, over 280yd in length and with arches up to 100ft in height, was the largest on the Central Wales.
G. M. Perkins courtesy C. C. Green

Right: Llandovery, where the CWER connected with the Vale of Towy Railway, with an up LNWR fish train headed by a Webb 4-6-0 four-cylinder compound of the 'Bill Bailey' class. The engine shed on the right is the property of the GWR; it was closed in 1935 and its engines transferred to the LNWR shed.
G. M. Perkins courtesy
C. C. Green

Below right: Llandilo, with a Carmarthen branch train in the bay platform headed by 2-4-2T No 465, with the usual three-coach branch sets. These sets lasted till the 1930s, while the 2-4-2Ts were still there at Nationalisation.
G. M. Perkins courtesy
C. C. Green

1859 the MT&AR had purchased Bailey's Tramroad which ran from the Nanty-Glo Ironworks to a wharf on the Brecon & Abergavenny Canal at Govilon and continued to Abergavenny along the Llanvihangel Tramroad — and it was in the process of converting the tramroads into a railway. Starting from a junction with the West Midland Railway at Abergavenny the first section of the MT&AR was opened to Brynmawr on 29 September 1862 with the LNWR making use of Shrewsbury & Hereford running powers over the erstwhile Newport, Hereford & Abergavenny Railway (that had been incorporated in the West Midland Railway in 1860) between Hereford and Abergavenny to gain access to the MT&AR. The line ascended from the River Usk at Abergavenny on an ever steepening gradient up the slopes of the Blorenge mountain, up through the Clydach Gorge at a gradient of 1 in 40 for the majority of the way. An extension to Nant y Bwch was opened on 1 March 1864, but the further extension towards Merthyr was fiercely contested by the Brecon and Merthyr Railway which company, having purchased the old 'Rumney Tramroad', was hoping to promote a railway from Merthyr to Nant y Bwch and then connect at Rhymney with the 'Rumney Tramroad'. The LNWR countered with a joint line with the Rhymney Railway between Nant y Bwch and Rhymney; this opened on 5 September 1871, with the use of running powers granted to Cardiff by the Rhymney Railway. From this date standard gauge wagons reached Cardiff directly without the delay and expense of transhipment to the broad gauge at Newport and in 1875 the LNWR opened its own Goods Depot at Tyndall Street Cardiff.

Having defeated the aspirations of the B&MR, the LNWR opened to Ivor Junction, on the B&MR's Dowlais branch, on 1 January 1873, thus enabling the company to compete for the traffic from the Ironworks there. After first obtaining powers to build its own line on into Merthyr, the LNWR compromised with the B&MR and built a line to the B&MR at Morlais Junction; the B&MR's line on to Rhydycar Junction became a joint B&MR-LNWR line; and, additionally, paid the B&MR half the latter's original costs for constructing this section of railway. Finally the trains of the LNWR ran through to Merthyr on 1 June 1879 and on

Right: Gowerton station was originally called Gower Road and was an original station of the Swansea extension with sidings to the Elba steel works and small collieries. It was also the junction for the Penclawdd branch. The photograph shows the view looking north, with the main line curving away to the right, beyond the level crossing the Penclawdd branch leading away to the left.
Courtesy Lens of Sutton

Below right: Penclawdd station with a branch passenger train headed by a 2-4-OT 'Chopper Tank'; the branch was built along the route of an earlier canal opened in 1814, was opened in 1871 and extended to Llanmorlais 10 years later. The Penclawdd branch passenger trains were an early casualty of grouping, being withdrawn in 1931, but the branch survived till 1952.
Courtesy G. Davies

4 May 1885 the LNWR opened their own station at Dowlais High Street. From that date the company ceased to use the B&MR station at Lloyd Street.

With the MT&AR running along the upper limits of the coalfield, the LNWR proceeded to promote a series of branch lines that tapped the valleys. The first one was the 1½-mile branch from Beafort to Ebbw Vale on a ruling gradient of 1 in 42; this was opened on 1 September 1867, and gave access to the iron and steel works there. A line built between Nantybwch and Tredegar was built under powers that the Sirhowy Railway obtained in 1860, along with powers to convert its tramway into a railway, and was opened on 2 November 1868. The Sirhowy Railway had opened negotiations with the GWR and the Monmouthshire Railway for the sale of its railway to these two companies, but these negotiations had foundered on the price to be paid. The LNWR made a better offer which the Sirhowy Railway accepted and thus the railway was leased to the LNWR from 13 July 1876. This gave the LNWR an alternative route to Newport and its docks, as well as to the expanding traffic of the Tredegar Iron Works and collieries. In

1869 a branch from Brynmawr to Blaenavon opened to goods traffic, giving access to the iron works and collieries; passenger services commenced on 1 January 1870. In 1877 the Blaenavon branch was extended to Talywain where a junction was made with the Pontypool-Abersychan branch of the GWR. A final joint line with the GWR was opened from Brynmawr to Nantyglo on 12 July 1905. Previously the LNWR had worked to the Rose Heywood Colliery over the line of the Nantyglo & Blaina Iron Co. The GWR extended its Western Valley passenger trains to Brynmawr to connect with the MT&AR trains.

None of the companies concerned owned any locomotives, except for the Knighton Railway which possessed a solitary Beyer Peacock 0-4-2T appropriately named *Knighton*. Standard Crewe types worked all services from the opening day over the Central Wales Line. The early passenger trains were worked by diminutive 2-2-0s, often in pairs, the goods trains being powered by Crewe pattern 2-4-0s. These were superseded by 2-4-0 'Precedents' and 'DX' 0-6-0 goods engines, which were often to be seen double-heading passenger trains. Shunting duties and local goods trips were

57

undertaken by Ramsbottom 0-4-0 and 0-6-0 saddle tanks. Webb 2-4-2Ts and 'Cauliflower' 0-6-0s assisted by 0-6-2 coal tank engines gradually replaced them on many duties, still working in pairs on the heavier trains. However in 1912 the Bowen Cooke 4-6-2Ts began to be drafted in — at last an engine had arrived for the semi-fast passenger trains that was ideal for the heavy gradients and enabled much double-heading and banking to be dispensed with. The Pacific tank engines were gradually displaced from 1928 onwards by the more modern Fowler 2-6-4Ts. The heavier coal trains were taken over by the 'GI' 0-8-0s, whose successors, the 'G2s', followed in early LMS days. Under the grouped companys, all the various Compounds that were rebuilt to these two classes were conveniently referred to as 'Super Ds'.

For the MT&AR's fearsome gradients, Ramsbottom built his special 0-6-0 saddle tanks to work goods and passenger trains. Some of the goods version were fitted for some time with the Le Chatelier 'Counter Brake', but its use was discontinued when badly scored cylinders resulted from careless application of the brake. Though Crewe engines were not noted for being particularly light on coal, the consumption on the

Right, top to bottom: Abergavenny Junction station on the old West Midland line was the smallest of three stations which Abergavenny used to possess. It was purely a junction with the MT&A section of the LNWR. Note that the train of LNWR coaches is still fitted with eyelets for the old exterior communication cord.
G. M. Perkins courtesy C. C. Green

The LNWR offices and shed were at Brecon Road station, the first station on the branch. The shed had at one time an allocation of over 40 engines. This one is the first Webb Compound 0-8-0 (originally No 50 but renumbered 2525 in 1894) with shed staff and enginemen.   *Courtesy S. Croall*

The backbone of all LNWR operations in South Wales was the 0-6-2T coal tank engines. Built to the usual Crewe standards, they were a bit flimsy for the duties they undertook, but they survived till nationalisation. Here is No 770, afterwards LMS No 7553.   *WRRC*

Govilon station in 1893, on the side of the Blorenge mountain where Crayshay Bailey's Llanvihangel Tramroad terminated at the wharf of the Brecon & Abergavenny Canal. Now the railway has gone but the canal still survives as a holiday route.   *Courtesy S. Croall*

Right: Gilwern station, where the railway climbed away from the Vale of Usk to enter the Clydach Gorge, marked the start of the stone quarries that remained the sole goods traffic when the through goods were diverted via Pontypool Road in 1954.
Courtesy Lens of Sutton

MT&AR was over double the rest of the LNWR at over 90lb per mile. The brake was not the strongest point of the Crewe design, but remarkably few runaway trains developed into serious accidents.

The 1876 leasing of the Sirhowy Railway involved the taking over of nine small tank engines, which were soon replaced by Crewe special tanks. From 1890 the 0-6-2T 'coal tanks', as they were usually known, took over most of the passenger and goods duties: at one time there were over 60 of them allocated to the MT&AR. They were assisted on the heavier trains by the 0-8-0 'Gl' tender engines and the 0-8-2 tank version. However at the end of LNWR days it appeared that the 0-8-4T, while very powerful and with plenty of weight on its coupled wheels, was a limited success because of its long wheelbase which distorted track. The MT&AR was a succession of curves and spirals, and these caused a lot of problems, leading eventually to the GWR banning them from the former Rhymney Railway on through trains to Tyndall Street goods depot. Excursions were often worked by the 0-8-0 tender engines or two coal tanks coupled, though on occasions various tender engines worked through from Hereford — usually 0-6-0 'Cauliflowers' and the Whale 4-6-0 '19in' goods engines or 'Experiment Goods' as they were locally known.

The local trains on the Central Wales line were latterly four-wheeled coaches displaced from the Birmingham suburban trains. A normal train consisted of two brake thirds, two thirds and a first composite lit with electric light. The Carmarthen and Penclawdd branches sets were of three coaches only, ie minus the two thirds. The through trains between Swansea and Shrewsbury, normally five trains a day, consisted of four bogie coaches some of which worked through from Shrewsbury to Manchester, Liverpool, Stafford and Euston.

The up Mail train in the evening conveyed a LNWR brake van that worked between Pembroke Dock and Manchester; also a 45ft brake composite working daily between Carmarthen and Manchester was extended to Pembroke Dock in the summer. This lavish service of through coaches was a result of attempts to develop traffic to the three Welsh Spas — Llandrindod, Llanwrtyd and Llangammarch Wells — where jaded businessmen could partake of the waters and cleanse their systems of the indulgences of past years. Unfortunately World War 1 saw the end of this traffic; the Welsh Spas were no longer the fashionable resorts of the day. Goods traffic on the Central Wales line consisted of anthracite and limestone products of the Amman valley, plus Swansea valley copper, steel and tinplate which required six trains a day to clear. One grave handicap the LNWR always laboured under was that they had no intermediate loop between Llandovery and Sugar Loaf Summit. This severely restricted the line capacity, as it was left to the LMS to make Cynghordy into a crossing loop in 1929.

The MT&AR was again worked by five coach sets of four-wheeled stock, the composites having first/second accommodation. From 1871 the LNWR provided through coaches from Liverpool and Manchester to Cardiff, despite the inconvenience of having to provide dual braked coaches because of the Rhymney Railway's adherence to the Westinghouse brake. These through coaches were withdrawn before World War 1 being superseded by the joint GWR-LNWR services from the West of England via the Severn Tunnel and the Shrewsbury & Hereford line. Only the through vans for parcel traffic from Liverpool and Crewe were running at Grouping. Through coaches also ran between Merthyr and Crewe with a Post Office sorting van from Euston to Merthyr daily.

59

The Sirhowy branch was the only LNWR branch were the major flow of traffic was down line either to Nine Mile Point to be transferred to the GWR or tripped to the Alexandra Docks of the ADR. At all other points the coal and steel had to be hauled up to the MT&AR over gradients like the pitch of a roof and despatched to Abergavenny and Hereford en route to the Midlands and the docks of Liverpool and Birkenhead where steam coal was always required by Mersey shipping interests. How successful they were can be judged by the fact that a third of the goods trains booked over the Shrewsbury & Hereford Railway were MT&AR trains. All coal shipment traffic was hauled up to the MT&AR to Rhymney Bridge and reached Cardiff Docks over the Rhymney Railway, though the Barry Railway successfuly diverted a considerable amount of this traffic to its own docks after 1905.

Above left: Brynmawr station, with the Nant y glo branch platform, was also the junction of the Blaenavon branch and industrial railways. The gradients of 1 in 34 eased slightly here to 1 in 66 before climbing to the summit at Beaufort Tunnel. *Courtesy Lens of Sutton*

Above: Tredegar was the most important station on the Sirhowy branch with its steel works and collieries. It had a four-road engine shed an an allocation of 25 locomotives to deal with this heavy mineral and slab traffic. Now it is but a memory. *Courtesy Lens of Sutton*

Below: Hollybush station in about 1920 with the coke ovens of the Tredegar Iron Co and colliery of E. D. Williams and his well advertised smithy coal. *Courtesy Lens of Sutton*

On 1 January 1923 the LNWR became part of the preliminary LMS group. But with the exception of the change of livery, it was many years before the Central Wales and the MT&AR lost their LNWR characteristics.

The Manchester & Milford Railway

The successor of several attempts to connect the industrial Midlands with the fine natural harbour of Milford Haven, the Manchester & Milford was incorporated by Act of Parliament dated 23 July 1860. It was to build a standard gauge railway from the Mid Wales Railway at Llanidloes down the Wye Valley to Llangurig then tunnel through the mountains to Yspyty Ystwyth and descend the Teifi valley through Tregaron and Lampeter to Pencader to connect with the broad gauge Carmarthen & Cardigan Railway. From here it was to lay a third rail on that railway to Abergwili Junction on the Llanelly Railway, with running powers into Carmarthen.

Construction began at the northern end in 1861 but because of disputes with the Llanidloes & Newtown and the Mid Wales Railways and its own precarious financial position, little real progress was made. An initial nine miles of railway to just beyond Llangurig was completed in 1863,

but then work was stopped while an attempt was made to obtain a deviation act to build a less costly railway through the mountains. Powers to build a branch line to Aberystwyth were first obtained under an act dated July 1861, but with rival schemes promoted by the Mid Wales Railway and a board of directors who were in conflict with each other, no more construction took place until David Davies and Frederick Beeston were given the contract to build between Pencader and Pontrhydfendigaid. Pencader to Lampeter was opened on 1 January 1866, a further section to Ystrad Meurig was completed

Below: The first passenger locomotives that the M&MR obtained were two standard Sharp Stewart 2-4-0 tender engines built in 1866. No 2 *Carmarthen* is as built except for the addition of a small cab and is seen here at Pencader before it achieved fame by a boiler explosion at Maesycrugiau in August 1890.
Courtesy National Museum of Wales

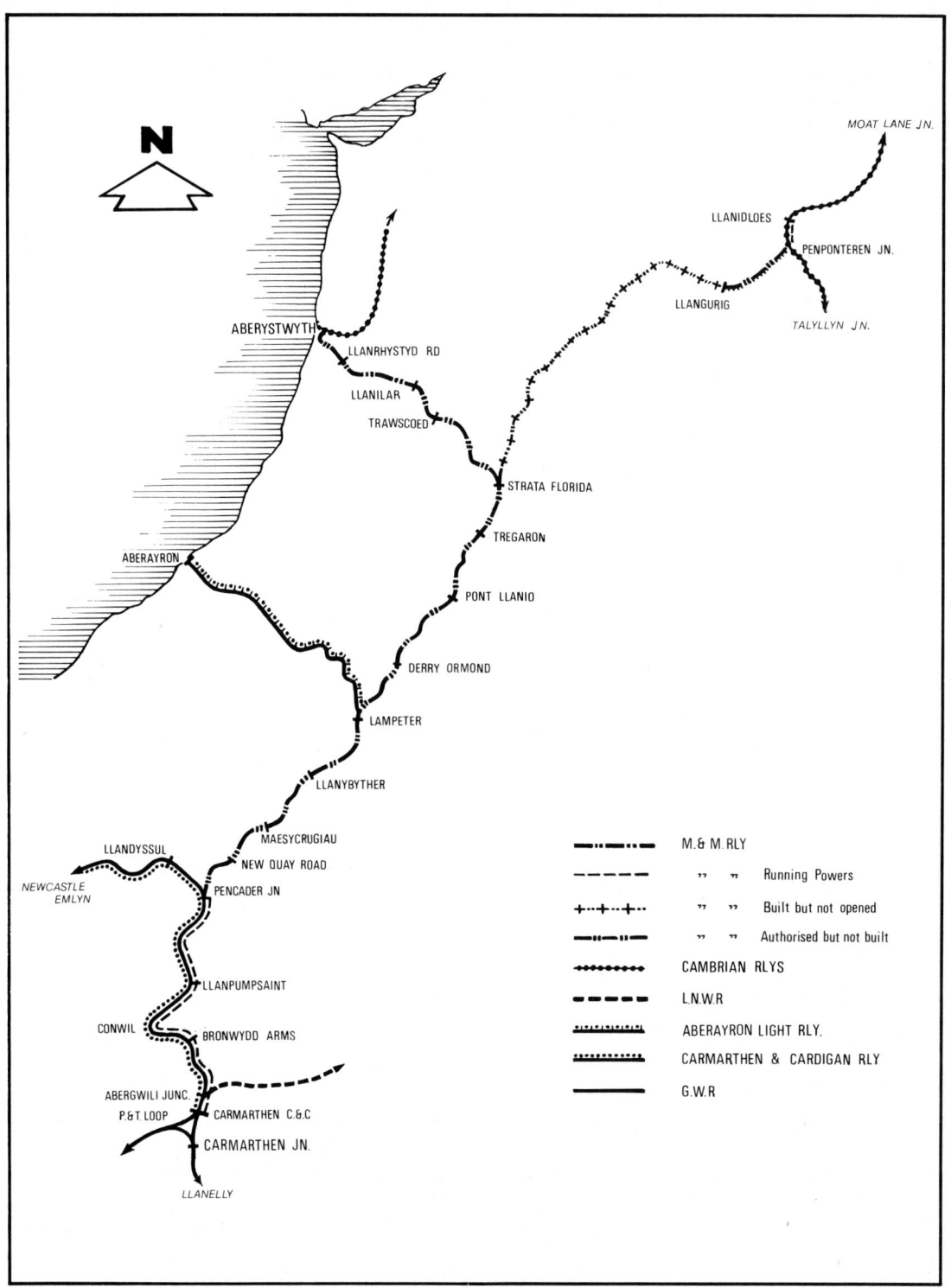

N

MOAT LANE JN.

LLANIDLOES

PENPONTEREN JN.

LLANGURIG

TALYLLYN JN.

ABERYSTWYTH

LLANRHYSTYD RD

LLANILAR

TRAWSCOED

STRATA FLORIDA

TREGARON

ABERAYRON

PONT LLANIO

DERRY ORMOND

LAMPETER

LLANYBYTHER

MAESYCRUGIAU

LLANDYSSUL

NEW QUAY ROAD

NEWCASTLE EMLYN

PENCADER JN.

LLANPUMPSAINT

CONWIL

BRONWYDD ARMS

ABERGWILI JUNC.
P.&T. LOOP

CARMARTHEN C.&C

CARMARTHEN JN.

LLANELLY

M.& M.RLY

" "   Running Powers

" "   Built but not opened

" "   Authorised but not built

CAMBRIAN RLYS

L.N.W.R

ABERAYRON LIGHT RLY.

CARMARTHEN & CARDIGAN RLY

G.W.R

in August 1866 and the laying of the third rail over the Carmarthan & Cardigan Railway was completed the same month, enabling through traffic to commence. An amended act of 1865 authorised a line from Ystrad Meurig (renamed Strata Florida) to Aberystwyth; this branch line to Aberystwyth was opened on 12 August 1867. This limited success was only possible because David Davies financed his own contracts, as the M&MR's always uncertain financial status had sunk even lower in the general uncertainty following the failure of the Quaker bankers, Overend and Gurney, the previous year.

However salvation was not far away, as John Barrow of the Staveley Coal & Iron Company, a director of the M&MR, bought the debenture shares that David Davies had received in part payment for constructional works and gained a majority holding in the M&MR. The Barrow family virtually financed the M&MR for the rest of its existence otherwise there is little doubt that it would have been abandoned, as was the Potteries and North Wales Railway.

Construction of the northern end of the main line ceased while the company tried to obtain a Deviation Act. This failed at the first attempt in 1864, and although a second Bill the next year was successful, no more construction ever took place because of a lack of funds.

So the M&MR settled down to working the local traffic between Aberystwyth and Carmarthen. Through coach working was instituted with the Pembroke & Tenby Railway. After the gauge conversion of 1872 when the GWR and its allies abandoned the broad gauge in Wales, the M&MR cut back its trains to Pencader — all through coaches and wagons being worked on by the Carmarthan & Cardigan Railway.

Left: A second goods engine was urgently required so John Barrow purchased an 0-6-0 locomotive from Manning Wardle in 1868. Not such a reliable engine as the Sharp Stewart products, it was nicknamed the 'old boat' on account of its rough riding qualities. Reboilered in 1891, it was cut up by the GWR in 1906.
J. E. Davies courtesy
C. C. Green

Centre left: At the time of *Carmarthen's* boiler explosion, four replacement boilers were under construction at the works of Sharp Stewart. The now spare boiler intended for No 2 was utilised to build a 2-4-2T. Delivered to the M&MR in 1891 and named *Plynlimmon*, the engine was allowed to wear itself out after the GWR take over and was condemned in 1916.
WRRC

Bottom left: The suitability of a tank engine to work the M&MR was soon apparent, so in 1896 the M&MR ordered a slightly larger version of *Plynlimmon*. This engine, No 6 *Cader Idris*, proved to be the last new engine the M&MR ever purchased and was the sole engine fitted with numberplates on its bunker sides.
Mrs Humphreys courtesy
C. C. Green

Right: *Cader Idris*, re-numbered 1306 by the GWR, did not stray far from its former area after grouping and soon took over the branch trains to Newcastle Emlyn. Many a Cardiganshire man took his first steps for war in 1914 with a journey behind *Cader Idris*. For the lucky survivors, *Cader Idris* was there to carry them home before it too became a casualty in April 1919.
Courtesy P. Korrison

As the M&MR had not paid its share of expenses for Llanidloes station and was also in arrears for Aberystwyth, the Cambrian and Mid Wales Railways obtained judgement against the M&MR for joint charges and it was placed in the hands of a receiver on 23 July 1875. The M&MR in its good years could pay its running costs and a limited amount of expenditure on maintenance, but the rent arrears for unpurchased land and debenture interest just accumulated year by year into an ever increasing mountain of liabilities. J. J. Barrow (the son of John Barrow) carried on after his father's death in 1871 and his own death in 1903 occurred in the midst of negotiations with the Cambrian and the GWR with the view of one of them taking over the M&MR. Though the Cambrian made a slightly better offer, the M&MR at the last minute came to terms with the GWR and signed an agreement with that company on 1 July 1905.

Because of the need to discharge the receiver and the opposition of the Cambrian, LNWR and Midland Railways, the GWR lease of the M&MR did not commence till exactly a year later, when most of the older members of the M&MR staff were discharged and GWR employees were drafted in. This was followed by the absorption of the M&MR by the GWR on 1 July 1907.

So the M&MR, of which such high expectations were forecast, was no more and the GWR had obtained an independent route to Aberystwyth.

The first locomotives recorded as working on the M&MR were Teifi, a Manning Wardle 0-6-0ST, and Montgomery, of which no particulars are known; both were the property of David Davies and were eventually removed by him.

The first locomotives the M&MR possessed were three Sharp Stewart standard products. The first, named General Wood, was an 0-6-0 tender engine; the other pair were 2-4-0 tender passenger engines named Carmarthen and Lady Elizabeth. These three engines were barely sufficient to maintain the limited services the M&MR operated and it is a measure of their good design and construction that they coped so well. No matter how short money was, it was obvious that additional motive power was required urgently. In 1867 John Barrow initially purchased a Manning Wardle 0-6-0ST similar to Teifi; Lampeter as it was named proved to be completely inadequate even for the light passenger trains. After a brief spell as a ballast engine during which the locomotive was used to lay the third rail on the Carmarthen & Cardigan Railway, the following year it was part exchanged with Manning Wardle for an 0-6-0 tender engine. Named Aberystwyth this engine was reputed to be equal with the Sharp Stewart General Wood. Aberystwyth proved to be a much more expensive engine to maintain and additionally it was very rough riding and lived up to its nickname of the 'Old Boat'.

The next arrival in 1870 was another Sharp Stewart 0-6-0 tender engine; always unnamed it became No 5.

The M&MR had to be content with these five locomotives and with the minimum of repairs they kept services going for over 20 years.

Replacement boilers became the necessity but were deferred year after year. Eventually an order for four replacement boilers was placed with Sharp Stewart but, before this could be implemented, No 2 *Carmarthen* blew up at Maesycrugiau on 19 August 1890, luckily with no loss of life. This was the end of *Carmarthen* and it was withdrawn and scrapped. A large portion of the boiler, which had landed in the River Teifi, was sold to a local scrapdealer on the understanding that the dome was brass; needless to say it was a standard Sharp Stewart steel product.

The immediate locomotive requirements were eased by hiring two engines from the GWR for £4 a day, a price the M&MR was unwilling to pay a moment longer than it needed to do so.

To replace *Carmarthen* the M&MR purchased an ex-LNWR 2-4-0 of the Allan Crewe type for £700; latterly LNWR No 3111, this was intended as a stop gap measure and was not numbered into M&MR stock. It proved to be a very useful little engine and was finally sold for scrap in 1900.

The other three Sharp Stewart engines were quickly reboilered before the end of 1891. The spare boiler intended for *Carmarthen* was used in a replacement engine built by Sharp Stewart. The new No 2 was a 2-4-2T delivered in 1891 and named *Plynlimmon*. It was a great success on all duties and quickly became a favourite. When the need for an additional engine became imperative in 1896 an enlarged version of *Plynlimmon* was ordered from Sharp Stewart, becoming No 6 *Cader Idris*, it was fitted with bunker side numberplates.

The 'Old Boat', No 4, was sent back to Manning Wardle for reboilering in 1897. There was serious thought about withdrawing it and obtaining a replacement. Indeed, in the event, with the cost of a new boiler, cylinders, fitting of vacuum brakes, and making other defects good, the final bill was not much less than the charge for a new engine.

Impressed with the ex-LNWR engine the M&MR purchased a LNWR 0-6-0 'coal' engine, latterly LNWR No 3561, built in 1889. This became M&MR No 7 and arrived on the scene in 1902. A similar engine, No 3088 built at Crewe in 1880, arrived in 1904 as a replacement for old No 1 *General Wood* which was withdrawn the same year.

To enable the M&MR to operate the improved Aberystwyth summer trains in 1905, the GWR loaned the M&MR three Dean Goods engines — Nos 2301, 2351 and 2532. To save any conflict with the Cambrian Railways about working into Aberystwyth, the were renumbered as M&MR Nos 8, 9 and 10 respectively.

After the working agreement with the GWR took effect in 1906, the majority of the M&MR stock was scrapped. No 2 *Lady Elizabeth* and her regular driver, Edward Benbow, were withdrawn the same day as he afterwards used to say.

Additionally Nos 4, 5 and 7 were withdrawn during the first year, leaving the last ex-LNWR 0-6-0 (renumbered 1338) to carry on coupled to a small GWR tender; with other GWR fittings it lasted in this hybrid state until 1915.

The two 2-4-2Ts became GWR Nos 1304 and 1306 respectively and both spent the majority of their life under the GWR working from Carmarthen and Pencader sheds. *Plynlimmon* was withdrawn in 1916; *Cader Idris* — the last survivor — settled down to work the Newcastle Emlyn branch trains. Many a 'Cardi' volunteer left home for the trenches of Flanders hauled by *Cader Idris*; for the lucky survivors the engine was still there to take them on the last stage of their journey home before it too made its final journey early in 1919.

The M&MR original coaches were 15 four-wheelers supplied by Ashbury's and the Midland Wagon Companies. Other wagons included a brake van, a horse box, and a carriage truck. The M&MR endeavoured to keep this modest stock in service with its limited workshop services. Three more coaches were added before 1890 when the M&MR reluctantly accepted the fact that the Board of Trade requirements for continuous brakes applied to the M&MR. The majority of the existing coaches were too decrepit to justify the cost of fitting these brakes, so the Barrow family came to the rescue and took up additional debenture shares to cover the cost of replacement bogie coaches. By 1895 these totalled six, seven of the original stalwarts being scrapped. In times of stress the M&MR used to hire coaches from the Cambrian and GWR for six shilling a day.

In the midst of the negotiations with the GWR in 1905, the M&MR purchased 12 ex-Mersey Railway four-wheeled coaches. The GWR

Left, top to bottom: After the GWR takeover, services were altered so that Aberystwyth trains ran through to Carmarthen while the former Carmarthen & Cardigan trains to Newcastle Emlyn became the branch and terminated at Pencader. The GWR also replaced the M&MR locomotives with Dean goods engines, one of which can be seen here at Conwill soon afterwards.
J. E. Davies courtesy C. C. Green

Dean goods No 2354 seen with a Carmarthen train at Tregaron; the leading coach is a slip coach of the Irish boat train from London working back to Carmarthen. Having been slipped at Carmarthen Junction, the coach was then worked by fast train calling only at Lampeter, running the whole journey in 126min to compete with the LNWR and Cambrian services from Euston.
J. E. Davies courtesy C. C. Green

The M&MR wayside stations were rudimentary, to say the least; here is Maesycrugiau in 1909 swamped with passengers from a Llanllwni Sunday school outing.
T. W. Evans courtesy C. C. Green

Trawscoed station looking towards Aberystwyth at the turn of the century. The crossing loop was for goods trains only — two passenger trains were not allowed to cross at Trawscoed. *Courtesy Lens of Sutton*

refused to accept these additions so they were sold off to other railways during 1906. The remainder the GWR took over, scrapping the non-bogie stock immediately. The bogie coaches were modified and altered by the GWR and the last of them was withdrawn in the 1930s from the Culm Valley branch in Devon.

The majority of the M&MR goods stock was made up of dumb-buffered open wagons, that they recorded as being built by themselves. With the addition of a few vans and cattle wagons fitted with sprung buffers, they were the best of the M&MR's efforts. A few vans and cattle wagons supplied by the Metropolitan Carriage & Wagon Co in 1899 were the most modern of the wagon stock handed over the GWR.

The M&MR wayside stations were small wooden buildings with whitewashed walls, and roofs felted and tarred. Llanybyther boasted a larger brick-built building, Lampeter — the principal station on the line — had a solid stone structure; both Llanybyther and Lampeter's buildings were renewals of the originals that had burnt down or rotted away.

The signalling equipment was supplied by Saxby & Farmer, each station having a small signalbox containing up to a dozen levers. With the addition of staff instruments and a small stove, they were rather cramped; most signalmen used to take their coats off before entering to ease matters a little.

The M&MR commenced its train services with three mixed goods and passenger trains a day. This indifferent service wandered up and down the track till 1880, when an extra train a day was put on. Though still mixed, these only conveyed through wagons — goods trains now conveyed the wagons for the wayside stations and did all the shunting. This transformed the M&MR services into a reliable and dependable little concern. The traffic was mostly of an agricultural nature, with the occasional load from the declining lead mining industry. The Cardigan, Coal, Lime Company (a subsidiary of the M&MR) had a depot at every station. The highspots for traffic were the monthly horse and cattle fairs at Llanybyther, Lampeter and Tregaron when up to 120 wagons of livestock would be loaded away. The M&MR had insufficient wagons to cope with these demands so the Cambrian and the GWR supplied stock on the understanding that the resultant traffic would be forwarded over their systems.

The GWR takeover saw the M&MR trains extended to Carmarthen, the former Carmarthen & Cardigan trains becoming the branch trains running only between Pencader and Newcastle Emlyn. The highlight of the passenger service was the slip carriage of the down 'Irish Boat Train' slipped at Carmarthen Junction and then coupled to the Aberystwyth train. This left Carmarthen at 1.25pm, calling only at Carmarthen Town, Lampeter and conditionally at Tregaron, and arrived at Aberystwyth at 3.40pm. This brave attempt to compete with the LNWR and Cambrian through carriages from Euston was a World War 1 casualty, never to be reintroduced.

So the Aberystwyth service settled down to four a day either way and pottered along like this down the years to the end.

The M&MR produced some fine railwaymen, among them J. W. Szlumper — afterwards resident engineer to the Barry, Vale of Rheidol and other railway extensions — his brother A. W. Szlumper, who became chief engineer to the L&SWR and Edmund Davies (the son of David Davies) who combined with James Metcalfe (formerly of the M&MR) to produce the internationally renowned Davies & Metcalfe steam injectors.

68

Top: A page from an early M&MR timetable.

Above: A commemorative banner is displayed in the Newtown Textile Museum recording the high hopes that the incorporation of the M&MR raised; alas, it was not to be. *Courtesy C. C. Green*

The GWR never revived any of the lapsed M&MR powers to build the original main line. The only additional railway constructed was the Lampeter, Aberayron & New Quay Light Railway — the final attempt to build a railway linking the small coastal ports with Aberystwyth. It was opened on 12 May 1911 from Aberayron Junction, a mile north of Lampeter, and ran down the Vale of Aeron to Aberayron. As it was constructed under the provisions of the Light Railways Acts, it followed the lie of the ground with some steep gradients and a series of ungated level crossings. It was worked by the GWR from opening and was finally absorbed by that company on 1 July 1922.

The Midland Railway in Wales

The western parts of Herefordshire and the adjoining portion of Brecknock were originally connected by the horse-drawn Hay Tramroad, opened between 1816-18. It ran from the wharf of the Brecon & Abergavenny Canal at Watton on the eastern side of Brecon through Talyllyn, Talgarth and Hay-on-Wye to Eardisley, where it made an end on connection with the Kington Tramroad which carried on to an ironworks at Kington.

Through the Railway Mania era of the 1840s the Wye Valley was part of the route of several trunk railways. No construction occurred until the Hereford, Hay & Brecon Railway was granted an act on 8 August 1859, and thus authorised to build a railway from a junction with the Shrewsbury & Hereford Railway, at Hereford, through Bronllys to a temporary terminus to the north of Brecon. From where extensions to Swansea and Milford Haven were envisaged. A tentative agreement was entered into for the Oxford, Worcester & Wolverhampton Railway and the Worcester & Hereford Railway to work the HH&BR as soon as 20 miles were open.

Because of boardroom disputes and wrangles, the first contractors — M'cormick and Holmes — soon gave up their contract and were replaced by Thomas Savin. Additionally the HH&BR obtained an amended act that permitted a junction with the Newport, Abergavenny & Hereford Railway and access to that company's Barton station at Hereford. The previous agreement with

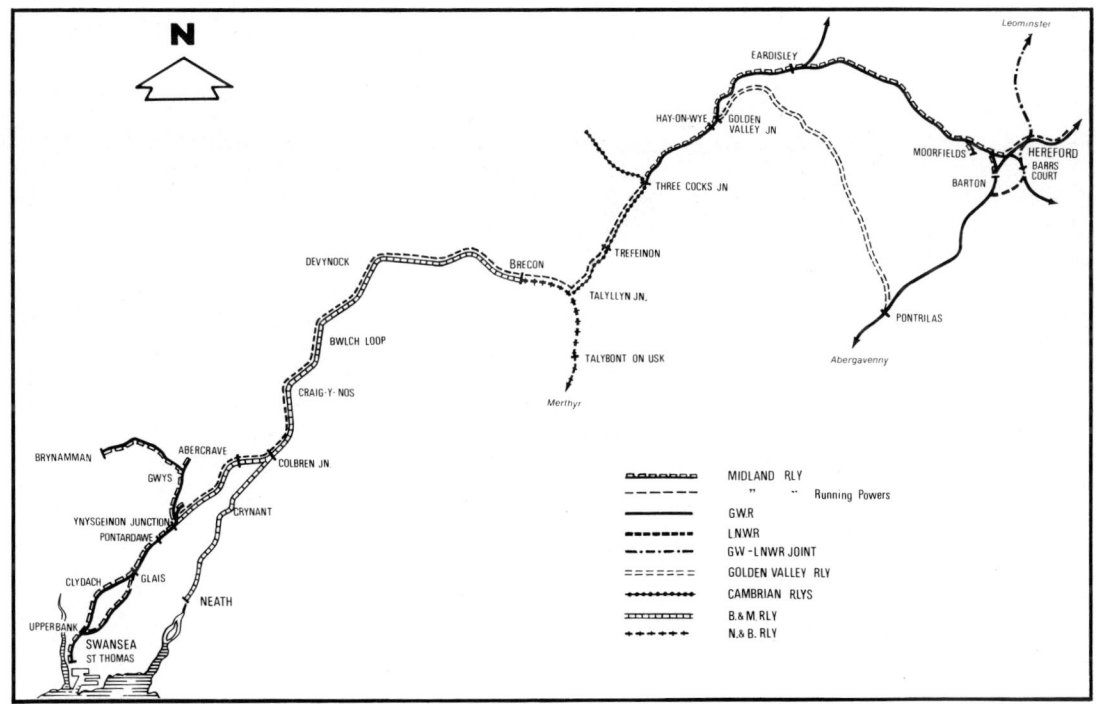

the OW&WR and W&HR was repudiated. On 6 November 1859 the HH&BR purchased the Hay Tramroad as an alternate route to Brecon, despite the objections of the Brecon & Merthyr and the Mid Wales Railways. The act of purchase was ratified with the amendments that the B&MR was allowed to purchase that portion of the Hay Tramroad between Talyllyn and Brecon, the Mid Wales that portion between Talyllyn and a junction with the HH&BR near an inn in the village of Aberllynfi. The inn, the 'Three Cocks', became the name of the junction station built here. Both the HH&BR and the Mid Wales Railway had unrestricted running powers into Brecon.

The first section of the HH&BR to be opened was for goods trains between Hereford and Moorhampton on 24 October 1862; a further extension to Eardisley followed on 30 June 1863. Passenger trains from a temporary terminus at Moorfields, Hereford commenced the same day. Services were extended to Hay on 11 July 1864 as the opening to Three Cocks Junction took place on 19 September 1864 when trains finally ran through to Brecon.

The HH&BR and the B&MR agreed to amalgamate, an act authorising this being implemented from 25 August 1865. Both railways were worked under contract by T. Savin. This amalgamation act was subsequently repudiated by the debenture share holders of the B&MR, who had never ratified it. The HH&BR resumed its separate existence from 13 July 1868 in the hands of a receiver because of unpaid debenture share interest: however, the receiver was discharged before the end of 1869. The B&MR ceased to work the HH&BR from 30 September 1868, when a temporary agreement with the Mid Wales Railway to work the latter for one year commenced.

The Midland Railway had running powers over the Worcester & Hereford Railway which had amalgamated with the Oxford, Worcester & Wolverhampton Railway and the Newport, Abergavenny & Hereford Railway in 1860 to form the West Midland Railway. Three years later the West Midland Railway amalgamated with the GWR. The lure of the rapidly expanding heavy industry of South Wales was irresistible to the Midland Railway which entered into an agreement to work the HH&BR in return for exclusive running powers. Starting on 1 October 1869, the first Midland train was denied access to Barton station by the GWR who blocked the junction with an engine and wagons. Moorfields station was hurriedly reopened and once again became the terminus for HH&BR services, while an arbitrator was appointed to settle the dispute. He confirmed the Midland Railway's right to inherit the HH&BR's running powers but the latter's trains did not use Barton station again till 1 April 1874.

After trying to lease the B&MR as a means of gaining access to Newport and Cardiff, the Midland Railway turned its attentions towards Swansea and leased the Swansea Vale Railway from 1 July 1874. The Swansea Vale Railway had been incorporated in 1855 to convert mineral tramroads in the Tawe Valley to build a railway to Pontadawe, and to build a Swansea Harbour branch of mixed gauge for the use of the broad gauge South Wales Railway and the Vale of Neath Railway. In 1856 a further act was obtained which allowed an extension to the iron works at Ynyscedwyn and also to join up with the horse-drawn Palleg tramroad at Ystalyfera.

A passenger service between Swansea and Pontadawe commenced on 24 February 1860. The SVR extended its services to Ynysygeinon on 21 January 1861, opening to Ystalyfera later the same year on 20 November 1861.

Meanwhile a further act, dated July 1861, authorised the extension to Brynamman over the lines of the Palleg and Cymllynfell tramroads; the conversion of this to a mineral railway was completed on 1 January 1864 as passenger trains were extended to Brynamman on 2 March 1868.

The final act the SVR obtained in 1867 enabled it to build the Morriston Loop Line to tap the traffic of Morriston and Clydach. This opened in stages the last one on 1 March 1875 after the Midland Railway's lease had commenced. From that date passenger trains began to run over the Morriston Loop, the old main line through Glais and Llansamlet becoming a goods line the same time. The Midland Railways offer to lease the SVR on very advantageous terms to the latter company, operated from 1 September 1874. This was followed by outright purchase in 1876.

Part of the promotion of the Swansea Vale & Neath & Brecon Junction Railway was to provide a direct standard gauge line between the N&BR and the SVR and both companies had exchanged running powers over each other's system. To the dismay of the N&BR, the Midland Railway — as inheritors of the SVR's running powers — informed the N&BR that it intended to inaugurate a through Hereford-Swansea service and would be exercising these powers between Brecon and Colbren Junction. Reluctantly the N&BR accepted the Midland Railway's offer to work all services between these points and pay the N&BR a third of the net receipts. The initial agreement was for five years and the Midland Railway's through service commenced on 2 July 1877.

The HH&BR handed over no locomotives to the Midland Railway — Savin had obtained two Sharp Stewart 2-4-0 tender engines to work the passenger services, but the B&MR had retained these in lieu of unpaid charges. The SVR locomotive stock was principally saddle tanks — five Sharp Stewart 0-6-0STs named after birds were the largest class. These were sent to shunt in Gloucester Docks by the Midland, where the survivors lasted till the early years of this century. As replacements the Midland Railway drafted in some of its standard 0-4-4T's to operate the passenger services, Nos 1734/35/36/37 apparently taking up these duties when built. They were replaced by Nos 1421/22/23/24 with larger water tanks and a boiler and firebox of more generous dimensions, which made them more suitable for climbing the gradients of the N&BR. The through goods trains became the duties of the Kirtley double-framed 0-6-0 tender engines of the '480' and '700' classes. But the real backbone of the Midland Railway's services were their South Wales tank engines, a development of the 0-6-0T half cab with a fully enclosed cab and a larger boiler and firebox. Built by Neilson's and the Vulcan Foundry, they took over all shunting and bank engine workings as well as the Brynamman branch passenger trains, working from Upper Bank shed at Swansea. With later additions to the class they survived to the end. The Midland Railway's locomotive operations were under the jurisdiction of a locomotive superintendent who was stationed at Brecon.

Below: The Midland Railway allocated four 0-4-4Ts Nos 1421/22/23/24 to haul the passenger trains between Hereford and Swansea. Fitted with larger boilers and water tanks, they appear to have had no difficulty in time keeping over the gradients they encountered; in fact one of them is reported to have arrived in Hereford in 1920 with seven six-wheel coaches and a four-wheel one for luck. No 1423 is in the yard at Brecon surrounded by most of the Midland Railway staff from the bowler-hatted locomotive superintendent downwards.
Courtesy T. Watkins

Above: For service in South Wales the Midland Railway brought out a variant of the standard half-cab 0-6-0T with an all over cab and larger boiler and firebox. Though primarily a goods engine these 'South Wales Tanks' as well as covering all bank engine workings also headed most of the passenger services on the Brynamman branch. Originally numbered 1102A to 1130, they were renumbered in the 1620 series. This photograph shows No 1103A on Brecon shed.   *WRRC*

Below: St Thomas station from the road in 1903. The Midland timetable for 1875 still called it Swansea SVR but it was not long before the name changed. St Thomas closed in 1950 when the Brynamman branch passenger trains were withdrawn.
G. M. Perkins courtesy C. C. Green

Top left: Pontadawe station in 1910 — an original SVR building which had survived from 1860. The mainstay of Pontadawe was goods traffic from Gilbertson Steel & Tin Works, a chemical works and four collieries.
Courtesy Lens of Sutton

Left: Ystrafera station seen pre-1914; the junction station for the Brynamman branch was opened by the SVR in 1861. Another important source of its traffic was the Gurnos Junction with the Yniscedwyn branch with collieries, tinmills, quarries and brickworks.
Courtesy Lens of Sutton

Below: Cwmllynfell, the last station on the Brynamman branch, was opened by the Midland Railway in 1896 as Gwaen-cae-Gurwen Platform. It was at the end of tramroads that extended — much to the disgust of the GWR — to the Gwaen-cae-Gurwen collieries.
Courtesy of Lens of Sutton

Right: Talgarth, with its low platforms and grey stone buildings of the former Mid Wales Railway, was the main crossing station on the quite busy single line between Talyllyn and Three Cocks Junctions. Proposals to double this seven-mile stretch were deferred and never carried out.
Courtesy Lens of Sutton

Centre right: The Midland Railway platforms at Three Cocks; the actual junction was 40 chains to the east to accommodate direct north to east junctions that were never installed. Three Cocks was named after a nearby inn of that name, instead of Aberllynfi the adjacent village.
J. Hobbs courtesy C. C. Green

Bottom right: Hay-on-Wye with its timber yards was the most prosperous market town on the HH&B section with double line between the station and the junction signalbox a quarter of a mile to the east. This was the point where the Golden Valley Railway meandered in from Pontrilas. Hopelessly in debt this railway was closed in 1898 and purchased by the GWR for a pittance. After refurbishing it was reopened in 1901. The three coach train of four-wheelers in the down platform marks one of its infrequent appearances from Pontrilas.
G. M. Perkins courtesy C. C. Green

Top far right: Eardisley was also the junction with the little GWR branch line through Lyonshall that connected at Titley Junction with the New Radnor and Presteign branches which left the Shrewsbury & Hereford line at Leominster. The GWR 0-6-0ST on the down line has arrived with one of the three or four trains a day that lingered on till 1941.
G. M. Perkins courtesy C. C. Green

The coaching stock of the SVR was supplied by W. Adams of Birmingham. The earliest introduced by the Midland were three-coach sets of four-wheelers, usually two brake thirds with a composite in between. Through coaches between Birmingham New Street, Worcester and Brecon commenced running on 8 July 1873, afterwards being extended to Swansea. On 2 January 1893 the Brecon and Barton Curve Junctions were brought into use; this allowed the Midland trains to use Barrs Court station and ended the through coaches being worked between Barton and Barrs Court stations by a little 0-6-0T. The Hereford-Swansea trains were now three-coach sets of six-wheeled coaches; on market days and Saturdays two sets of coaches were coupled together to cater for the additional traffic. The through coaches to Birmingham were 40ft bogie brake composites. The through coaches were temporarily withdrawn from 31 December 1916, never to be reintroduced. The LMS, as successors of the Midland, withdrew their passenger trains between Brecon and Colbren Junction on 31 December 1930. But the Brynamman branch trains ran a connecting service between Ynysygeinon and Colbren until 12 September 1932 when this service was withdrawn and the LMS confined its passenger operations to the Swansea-Brynamman local trains.

While the Midland Railway's passenger receipts were not very high and its through coaches a source of annoyance to the GWR and LNWR, the freight traffic was heavy and rewarding. With its policy of competing vigorously for the copper and other metallic products of the Swansea valley by payments of generous rebates to other railways, additional traffic was attracted to the Midland route. Other traffic came from the anthracite workings from collieries on the Brynamman branch which required seven through trains a day. Gradients were very steep between Ynysygeinon and Devynock and this restricted mineral trains to 18 wagons. The train required an assistant engine in the rear to the Bwlch Summit Loop, where the assistant engine was placed on the front of the train engine to help control the train on the now falling gradient to Devynock. These trains required two brake vans; the second one with an assistant guard was placed in the middle of the train. All this made it an expensive piece of railway to operate, though the easier gradients over the HH&BR enabled trains to make up to 30 loaded wagons leaving Talyllyn for Hereford.

Some of the original stations of the SVR survived to the end of services, aided with a few additions of the Midland Railway. The HH&BR stations were of timber clap boards except for Westmoor, a private station between Moorhampton and Credenhill, which was a substantial brick-built structure with living accommodation for an attendant.

The whole of the Midland Railway's route to Swansea was single line except for crossing loops and a short stretch of double line from Brecon Junction to Mount Street Brecon; in all there were 26 tablet sections to pass through.

The Pooling Of Traffic Agreements between the four railways in 1932 to eliminate wasteful competition sounded the death knell for all that the Midland Railway had built up. The through goods trains were withdrawn in September 1932, this traffic henceforth being forwarded over the Vale of Neath line of the GWR.

The Neath & Brecon Railway

This railway was originally incorporated as the Dulais Valley Railway, by an act of Parliament dated 29 July 1862. Its brief was to build a standard gauge railway between collieries in the Dulais Valley and a junction with the then broad gauge Vale of Neath Railway at Cadoxton (Neath) and, additionally, to lay a third rail on the latter to gain access to Neath and the Swansea docks if the Vale of Neath Railway did not lay the third rail themselves.

The first section from Neath to the Drim Colliery at Onllwyn was opened on 2 September 1864. Meanwhile the ambitions of the Dulais Valley Railway had expanded and by means of an additional act, dated 13 July 1863, it had changed its title to the Neath & Brecon Railway.

It now had powers to extend northwards over the mountains to Devynock, thence along the Vale of Usk to Brecon where a junction with the Hereford, Hay & Brecon Railway was to be made. A further act, dated 29 July 1864, authorised a mineral line from Onllwyn to Maes-y-Marchog and a branch line from Devynock to Llangammarch Wells on the Central Wales Extension Railway of the LNWR.

The Onllwyn to Brecon section opened to a temporary station at Mount Street Brecon on 8 June 1867; on the grand opening day the service was worked by an engine borrowed from the Vale of Neath Railway. Differences with the Brecon & Merthyr Railway, that were not entirely resolved until 1874, prevented the N&BR

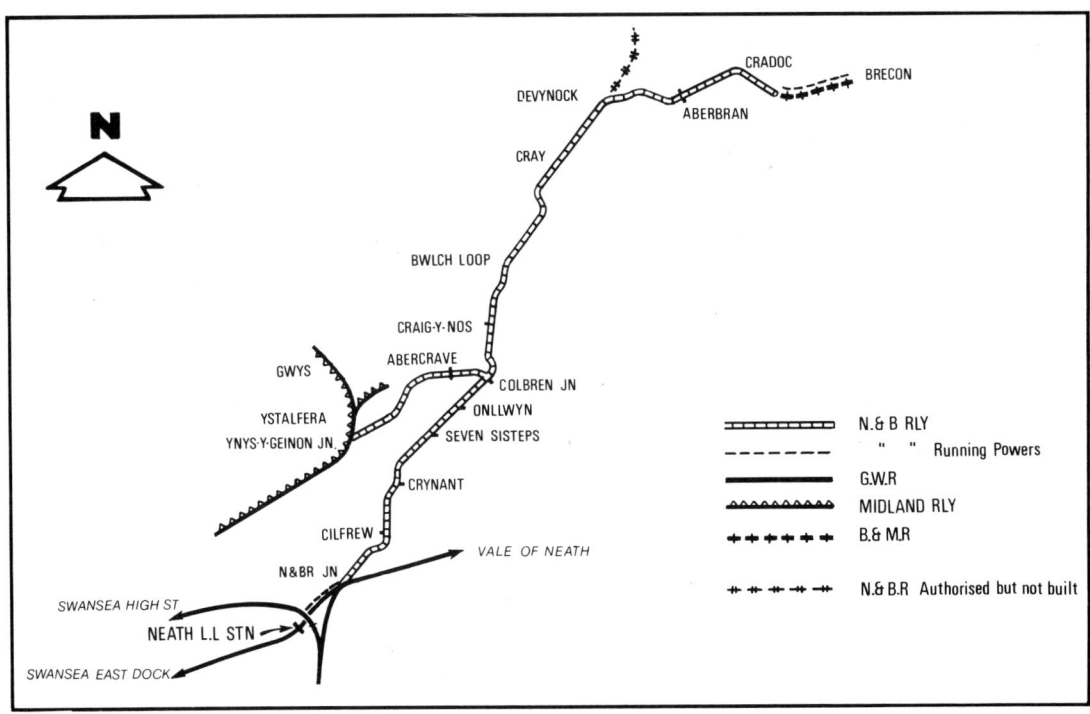

trains running into that company's stations. Through passengers were ferried between the two stations on the footplate of the N&BR engines and, in fact, until 30 April 1871 the Mid Wales used Mount Street as its Brecon terminus.

Initially John Dickson, the contractor who built the N&BR was also contracted to supply locomotives and rolling stock and operate the train services. The earthworks for over five miles of the Llangammarch branch were completed, but no permanent track was laid before construction ceased in the uncertainty and loss of confidence following the failure of the bankers Overend and Gurney in 1866. This was followed by the failure of John Dickson in 1868 and, thus, the end of his aspirations to extend the N&BR to Swansea and Mumbles Head — where he intended to build a shipping stage — by means of running powers over the Oystermouth Railway.

The N&BR extension to Brecon was a very expensive railway to operate, with little traffic from the wayside stations, and the N&BR was in the unhappy position of having its expenditure exceed its receipts by £500 a year. In a desperate attempt to rectify this adverse position, the N&BR absorbed the Swansea Vale & Neath &

Brecon Junction Railway on 26 July 1869. This railway was authorised by an act dated 29 July 1864 to build a railway from Colbren on the N&BR to an end on junction with the Swansea Vale Railway at Ynysygeinon. Opened on 10 November 1873, this gave the N&BR running powers to Swansea and in return the Swansea Vale Railway enjoyed running powers over the N&BR to Brecon.

By now the financial plight of the N&BR was desperate. The shares issued totalled nearly £1,500,000 — most of them in the form of debenture shares with enhanced rates of interest — and of this a mere £10,000 was available for distribution.

Much to the dismay of the N&BR, the Midland Railway, having reached Brecon by its agreement with the Hereford, Hay & Brecon Railway leased the Swansea Vale Railway on

Below: Normally the N&BR did not work north of Colbren Junction, however No 4 here is seen at Sennybridge attached to the GWR's Divisional Engineer's saloon borrowed for the occasion of a director's inspection trip. With the exception of ballast and engineering trains, the Midland Railway operated all other services. *WRRC*

1 September 1874, and then intimated that it intended to run through trains over the N&BR using the SVR's running powers. The N&BR was in no position to contest the issue and very reluctantly accepted the Midland Railway's offer to work all main line services between Brecon, Colbren and Ynysgeinon and pay the N&BR one third of the net receipts. Initially this was about £4,000 per annum, and this modest additional amount of money gave a 20% increase in net receipts. The agreement took effect from 1 July 1877 for an initial five years and the N&BR confined their train services to the Neath Colbren branch.

The agreement was renewed up till 1889 when the N&BR, at the instigation of their Chairman Sir Edward Watkin, attempted to obtain more favourable terms from the Midland Railway. In the midst of negotiations the Midland arrogantly withdrew its through trains on 20 June 1889 and diverted them over the Vale of Neath line of the GWR. Sir Edward Watkin, who among his many railway interests was additionally Chairman of the Manchester, Sheffield & Lincolnshire Railway, arranged for locomotives, rolling stock and train crews to restore services on the N&BR. Leopold Ahrons in his *Locomotive and Train Working of the 19th Century* stated that MS&L locomotives and rolling stock only supplied a meagre service. This is incorrect as is shown in a Board of Trade accident report of a minor derailment to a passenger train on the N&BR at this time which indicates that the crew of this train were MS&LR employees. In the end the N&BR asked an arbitrator to settle the differences with the Midland Railway and that railway resumed working the through trains over the N&BR from 22 July 1889. The N&BR had been awarded an enhanced annual payment and compensation against the Midland Railway for the inconvenience caused.

From 1890 the N&BR began to enjoy a modest prosperity and after purchasing additional locomotives and rolling stock started to work the coal trips between Colbren and Ynysgeinon from 1 July 1903. By 1913 the coal traffic conveyed by the N&BR had increased to 1,200,000 tons a year.

The first locomotives used by the N&BR appear to have been supplied by the contractor, John Dickson, who contracted to work the line from 29 September 1866. After the failure of Dickson in 1868 the stock was hired from T. B. Forward. Ultimately the N&BR purchased all its rolling stock — probably in 1871 when it began showing rolling stock in the Directors' Reports to the Shareholders.

Dickson supplied a Fairlie Patent engine named *Progress* — an 0-4-0+0-4-0T built by J. Cross of St Helens in 1865. Regrettably the performance of *Progress* left a lot to be desired; as with all these engines, the steam joints between the power bogies and the boiler were impossible to keep steam tight. T. Forward informed Dickson that the N&BR did not wish to hire *Progress* any longer as soon as he assumed control in 1868. After attempting to sell the engine by auction, it was given to G. England of Hatcham Works to clear outstanding debts of Dickson and the N&BR.

A second Fairlie was bought by Dickson from the Anglesey Central Railway, another of his contracts, in 1866. Also built by Cross and named *Mountaineer,* again an 0-4-0+0-4-0T, it was a smaller engine than *Progress* and did little work on the N&BR, being reported lying out of use at Cadoxton yard in 1869. It was finally sold for £100 in 1880 having done little work since 1868.

For the passenger services Dickson obtained from George England two 2-4-0 tender engines which were originally intended for the Somerset & Dorset Railway but cancelled because the S&D not pay for them. Named *Neath* and *Brecon*, they did little work after the working agreement with the Midland Railway, started in 1877 and were in Cadoxton yard until sold for £350 in 1884 and were cut up.

A little 0-6-0 well tank engine appeared on the N&BR, transferred from the Anglesey Central Railway. It was named *Miers* after R. H. Miers, the first Chairman of the N&BR. With wheels of only 3ft 6in diameter, it was used for shunting and yard duties until sold for £100 in 1882.

By 1870 the locomotive situation was desperate: only the two England 2-4-0s were fit for traffic and locomotives had to be hired from the Midland and Mid Wales Railways to keep services running. When a new engine arrived in 1871 it was surprisingly a 4-4-0T passenger engine from the Yorkshire Engine Co. Eventually numbered 4, it became the principal passenger

Top left: Increasing traffic compelled the N&BR in 1899 to obtain two 0-6-0STs from Nasmyth, Wilson & Co. One of them, No 8, had a heavy repair at Swindon in 1916 and came back into traffic with a full length saddle tank, GWR pattern coal bunker, smokebox and chimney. Seen after taking water in 1921, No 8 did not last long after grouping, being withdrawn in 1927
G. H. W. Clifford courtesy C. C. Green

Left: In 1908, whilst awaiting delivery of a batch of three modern 0-6-2Ts, the N&BR purchased an 0-6-0ST from the GWR. Three more were obtained in 1911, and here former GWR No 1563 renumbered as NBR No 14 is seen shunting at Neath in 1921. No 14 had been reboilered in 1920 by the Avonside Engine Co.
G. H. W. Clifford courtsey C. C. Green

Below: A Midland Railway down passenger train halted at Sennybridge in 1905; the two through coaches a day from Birmingham to Swansea provided a much appreciated service. The train engine is one of the regular 0-4-4 Ts.
Courtesy T. Watkins

Above: 'South Wales Tank' No 1106A on a pick up goods working at Sennybridge complete with staff and four legged supervisor. The second wagon on the train is a rare example of a N&BR van in service.
Courtesy M. E. Morton Lloyd

Right: To break the long block section between Sennybridge and Craig-y-Nos, the N&BR built a crossing loop at Bwlch. This lonely outpost nestling below Fan Gihirych was 1,254ft above sea level and marked the highest point on the N&BR. Here trains ceased to blast their way upwards and began a cautious descent with squeaking brakes trying to restrain the train.
Courtesy T. Watkins

Below right: Because of the isolated situation of the Bwlch Crossing Loop which was remote from any road access as no passenger trains called there, the N&BR management provided a pair of goats so that the signalman's children could have a daily supply of fresh milk. In the run down of the N&BR section after the through goods trains were withdrawn in 1932, the GWR abolished Bwlch Loop. I wonder what they did with their now redundant servants? Where were they transferred to?. *Courtesy T. Watkins*

engine of the N&BR for the rest of its days. After Appleby had been appointed consultant to the N&BR, two double-framed 0-6-0STs arrived in 1873, These were enlarged versions of previous engines that H. Appleby had built for the Monmouthshire Railway. They impressed the N&BR with their capabilities and a further pair was ordered. Later this order was increased to four and their arrival in 1874 gave the N&BR a reliable stock of locomotives that could handle its traffic competently. Unfortunately the working agreement with the Midland Railway rendered some of these engines surplus to the N&BR restricted requirements, so two of the 0-6-0ST's were sold to the Brecon & Merthyr Railway in 1877 for £1,500 each, much to the sorrow of the N&BR locomotive foreman who wished to retain them. The four the N&BR retained were afterwards fitted with the vacuum brake and all over cabs enclosing the coal bunkers. Two were withdrawn before grouping but the other two were handed over to the GWR.

After the Swansea Vale & Neath & Brecon Junction Railway was opened an additional passenger engine was purchased. Formerly the Monmouthshire Railways No 14A, this 2-4-0T turned out to be useless and was sold to the Hoylake & Birkenhead Railway in 1879 at a loss.

The existing locomotive stock was adequate until 1892 when a 2-4-0T, identical to the Class C of the Barry Railway, was purchased. Fitted with the vacuum brake from new, this locomotive's arrival enabled the 4-4-0T to be so fitted and some urgent repairs to be carried out.

Increased coal traffic saw the appearance of two 0-6-0STs from Nasmyth Wilson; except for their inside frames they were otherwise similar to Nos 1-4.

When the N&BR took over the goods trips between Colbren and Ynysygeinon in 1903, it purchased two of the Port Talbot Railway's surplus 0-6-2Ts; only five years old they were a big advance on the remainder of the locomotives. Reboilered at Swindon with Belpaire boilers supplied by the makers in 1912 and 1913, they were probably the best bargain the N&BR ever made.

Three further 0-6-2Ts similar to the Rhymney Railway's 'M' class were delivered in 1906 and 1908 — they were the last new engines the N&BR ever purchased.

Between 1908 and 1914 the N&BR purchased four second-hand GWR 'Buffalo' class 0-6-0STs to supplement the original Appleby engines which were now coming to the end of their days. With the exception of one scrapped in 1922, the remainder resumed their former GWR numbers after grouping.

J. Dickson provided four third class and three composite carriages to commence the passenger train services; these were replaced and added to through the years by other mostly second-hand carriages. In later years a good source of four-wheeled coaches came from railways carrying out suburban electrification schemes. Even then the N&BR tended to buy from the cheaper end of this market. At the grouping the company had stock from the Hull & Barnsley as LSWR, as well as some of undisclosed parentage. The majority of these bargains were hurriedly withdrawn by the GWR.

The passenger service consisted of five trains a day (six on Saturdays) between Neath Riverside and Colbren Junction; the first up and down trains were mixed goods and passenger trains and only ran to Onllwyn.

When Madame Adelina Patti — a much respected celebrity — purchased Craig y Nos estate and used it as a retreat between her singing engagements, special trains to and from Penwyllt resulted. Both the GWR at Neath and the Midland at Swansea always had a saloon available so that the N&BR could provide her with a carriage suitable for her requirements. Additionally the N&BR renamed Penwllt station Craig y Nos and when they rebuilt it they provided a private waiting room for Madame Patti.

Dickson supplied 20 open wagons and 15 vans with which to start goods services; however, thankfully for the company, most of the traffic originating on the N&BR was either coal or stone and was conveyed in the private owner wagons of the supplier or of a shipping agent. In 1922 the N&BR handed over to the GWR 85 opens, 11 vans, 8 cattle wagons, 10 timber trucks, 6 goods brake vans, 12 ballast wagons and a travelling hand crane.

The station buildings were originally built of timber clapboard cladding, some with a distinctive rounded roof reminiscent of an old gipsy caravan — Colbren and Crynant were of this pattern. Several stations, including Devynock and

Left: David James and workmate at Seven Sisters dressed in N&BR uniform with waistcoats that buttoned up to the neck and soft topped caps. The blue enamelled station sign with white letters was usual on the N&BR. *Courtesy M. E. Morton Lloyd*

Below: The Dulais Valley, in contrast to the Vale of Usk, was a scene of industrial activity with quarry, tinmills and collieries. Amongst these valuable sources of traffic to the railway was the Evans and Bevan colliery at Seven Sisters. *Courtesy M. E. Morton Lloyd*

Bottom: A photograph of Colonel Bevan himself, famous colliery proprietor and brewery owner (the brewery survived till taken over in recent years) with the late David James (that mine of information on the N&BR) together in Seven Sisters Colliery sidings. *Courtesy M. E. Morton Lloyd*

Craig y Nos, were rebuilt in local stone. Between Aberbran and Devynock were the private stations of Abercamlais and Penpont, both for the exclusive use of the two estates. As the stations were painted brown and cream the likeness to the Midland Railway was heightened.

The original signalling equipment was supplied by Duttons, but when that firm's interests were taken over by McKenzie & Holland they continued to supply the N&BR with the Dutton pattern signals — the N&BR was one of the few Welsh railways not to adopt the somersault signal. Tyers No 4A tablet instruments were used to control trains over this single line railway.

The end of the road came for the N&BR on 24 July 1922 when it was absorbed by the GWR. The pattern of services was little altered until the LMS, as successor to the Midland Railway, withdrew its through Hereford-Swansea trains on 31 December 1930, when the GWR introduced Brecon to Neath trains.

Left Crynant station and staff in 1920; the N&BR had several stations built of timber with a clap-boarded exterior and a distinctive rounded roof profile somewhat reminiscent of a gipsy caravan. Alas they have been destroyed since the railway closed.
Courtesy M. E. Morton Lloyd

Below: Cilfrew signalbox and crossing loop was half a mile from the passenger station of that name. There was controlled entry to the tinmill sidings and Tyrisaf Quarry.
Courtesy T. Watkins

Bottom: The station staff at Sennybridge in 1905; this station was at different times called Devynock, Devynock & Sennybridge, and Sennybridge & Devynock.
Courtesy M. E. Morton Lloyd

The Port Talbot Railway

Last but not least of the Welsh railways to be promoted was the Port Talbot Dock and Railway Company. Spurred on by the success of the Barry Railway, the dock and railway would be under a single management team and most of the principal shareholders would be the coal owners and industrialists who would be the main customers.

The small dock at the mouth of the River Afan was built in 1835-37 by Emily Charlotte Talbot, after whom the undertaking was named. Connected by several tramroads to copper works, iron works and collieries it was the only small dock between Barry and Swansea where development was possible.

The PTD&R was incorporated by an act of Parliament dated 31 July 1894, to acquire the existing dock and build a new one with improved facilities. It was empowered to construct a railway from the docks through Port Talbot to Dyffryn Yard where a locomotive shed and workshop was to be built. From there it was to climb the valley to the Bryn on a gradient steepening to 1 in 40, pass through the Cwm Ceren tunnel and drop down to Maesteg in the Llynfi valley. From here, after encircling Maesteg in a spiral, it would climb again to Lletty Brongu, descend to a junction with the Gawr Branch of the GWR at Pontyrhyll, then by means of running powers granted, gain access to

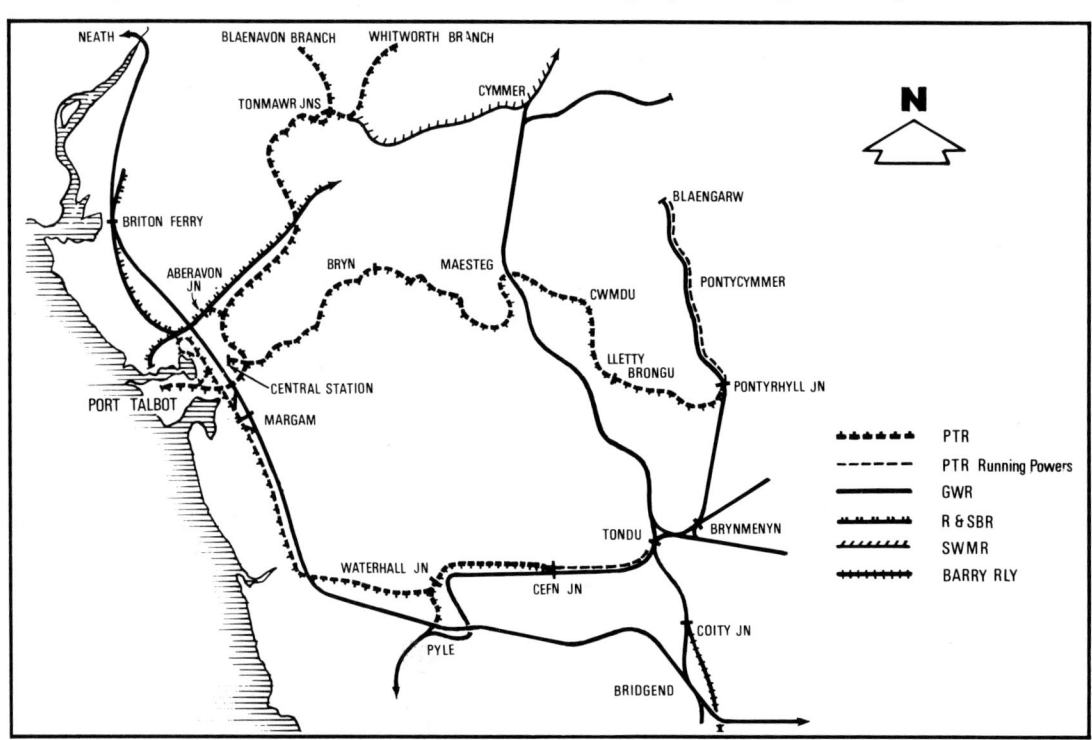

Blaengarw at the head of the valley. Also included there was a short line from Dyffryn Junction to the R&SBR at Averavon and to the passenger terminus of the PTR which was known as Port Talbot Central station.

Construction started straight away on the new dock and the main line, with its heavy gradients, tunnel and 11 bridges and viaducts. Train services commenced to Lletty Brongu on 31 August 1897; the remainder of the main line to Pontyrhyll was opened on 17 January 1898.

The PTR obtained an act to build the Ogmore Valleys Extension Railway on 20 July 1896. In complete contrast to the remainder of the PTR it ran parallel to the main line of the GWR with which it connected at Margam Junction: then on a rising gradient of 1 in 200 it crossed over the GWR and connected with the Cefn & Pyle Railway at Waterhall Junction. The PTR purchased the Cefn & Pyle Railway on 1 January 1897 and inherited its running powers from Cefn Junction to Tondu. The Ogmore Valleys Extension Railway was opened on 19 December 1898.

The other line authorised under an act of 1896 was for a mineral railway from Tonygroes Junc-

tion running up the Afan Valley crossing over the R&SBR below Pontrhydyfen and heading on up the Pelena Valley where a junction was made at Tonmawr with the Blaenavon and Whitworth branches of the South Wales Mineral Railway. This was opened for traffic on 14 November 1898, and from that date the PTR took over the two branches from the SWMR giving the collieries an improved outlet at Port Talbot. Finally the PTR took over the SWMR from 30 March 1908.

The first years of the PTR were difficult. The contractors did not complete the docks until early 1901, with a capacity of 3,000,000 tons, trade slowly built up from 500,000 tons a year initially to 850,000 tons by 1906. The same year the

85

Right: Like most Welsh railways the PTR started services with 0-6-2T locomotives but these were found wanting on the heavy gradients of the PTR. So in order to reduce bank engine mileage, the PTR in 1900 placed an order with Sharp Stewart for three 0-8-2Ts. Similar to the 'H' class of the Barry Railway (W. J. Hosgood the PTR Locomotive Superintendent having previously been assistant to his brother J. H. Hosgood Locomotive Superintendent of the Barry Railway) these had larger fireboxes, shorter boilers and other detail differences. They were soon blasting their way up the Bryn in their chocolate livery en route to Maesteg and the Gawr collieries. Here in 1914 is No 18 at Dyffryn Yard receiving attention from the cleaners. *WRRC*

Below right: Because of the inability of British locomotive manufacturers to supply engines within a reasonable period of time, in 1899 an order was placed in the USA with the Cooke Locomotive Co for two 0-8-2Ts. With bar frames, and drumhead smokeboxes, they were a mixture of American and British practices. As soon as the GWR took over the PTR, G. J. Churchward reboilered them but unfortunately he sat his firebox on top of the bar frames which restricted the depth of the firebox and did nothing to assist firemen when working up the 1 in 40 gradients of the PTR. Here is No 21 after being reboilered at Swindon. *Courtesy A. Rees*

ordinary shareholders had their first dividend. Working expenses were *53:75%*, the tonnage of coal continued to increase as the Elder Dempster shipping line began loading all the steam coal they required for bunkerage around the world.

The PTR had overtures made to it by the Barry Railway as part of that company's attempts to gain access to the Swansea Valleys. But as it had an investment in a dock that was working well below capacity, the directors of the PTR did not like the idea of a project that was likely to divert traffic away from their £500,000 docks. At the same time, the GWR, determined to thwart the ambitions of the Barry Railway, made a very attractive offer to the PTR. By this the PTR retained control of the docks while the GWR worked the railway and guaranteed the dividends that the directors recommended to the shareholders. The PTR accepted the GWR's offer and the working agreement was implemented from 30 March 1908. Within a few years

the ordinary dividend of the PTR reached 9% which it maintained till 1922.

The only oddities in the PTR locomotive stock were the three engines taken over from the Cefn & Pyle Railway. The first, *Derby* a Fox Walker 0-6-0ST, was sold the same year, 1897. The second, *Bryndu No 3* a 0-4-2ST, had been sold to the Bryndu Colliery by the GWR in 1873 and was also sold by the PTR in 1897. The third engine, *Penylan* a Manning Wardle 0-6-0ST built in 1886, lasted on the PTR until 1908 when the GWR scrapped it. The PTR hired out a locomotive to the Gwendraeth Valley Railway during 1905-6 after that company had terminated its agreement with the BPGVR to work its line, pending the arrival of its own engine. The only PTR engine identified on hire to the GVR is *Penylan* and was probably the only engine involved in this hire.

The PTR commenced its services with 11 0-6-2Ts for its coal trains; these were built by R.

Right: For shunting in the docks and trip workings, Hudswell Clarke supplied the PRT with a class of six 0-6-0STs similar to three others obtained for the opening of the railway. They were powerful engines and an immediate success, Here is No 25 as built, on shed at Dyffryn Yard; afterwards the engine was sold to the Varteg Colliery at Pontypool and lasted till 1950. *WRRC*

Stephenson & Co in 1897-8. Though successful, experience proved that a more powerful engine would reduce the need for banking assistance. After the arrival of the 0-8-2Ts four of the 0-6-2Ts were sold, two to the R&SBR in 1901, two to the N&BR in 1903.

For trip working and shunting around the docks, a powerful 0-6-0ST was adopted; three arrived from R. Stephenson in 1898, a further six practically identical were supplied by Hudswell Clarke in 1901. One of these engines is at the moment on the Severn Valley Railway awaiting restoration.

For the passenger services, W. J. Hosgood, the first Locomotive Superintendent (previously he had been assistant to his brother J. H. Hosgood the Barry Railway Locomotive Superintendent) purchased from the Barry Railway two Sharp Stewart 2-4-0s that were surplus to the Barry requirements. The first one, No 37 arrived in 1898; the second one, Barry Railway No 52, was rebuilt to a 2-4-2T identical to the Barry's rebuilds and arrived in 1899. It was renumbered No 36. With brass numerals on their chimneys and in a red brown livery with cream lining, they were little altered from their Barry days.

To overcome the deficiencies of the 0-6-2Ts on the heavy gradients of the PTR, more powerful goods engines became an urgent requirement. At the time British manufacturers had full order books so the PTR turned to an American manufacturer. In 1899 the Cooke Loco Co of New Jersey supplied two 0-8-2Ts with many American features; bar frames, taper boilers and drumhead smokeboxes. At the same time the Barry Railway was also having locomotives built in America, so that company supervised the PTR order which on completion was shipped to Barry

Docks and assembled there. Starting work on the PTR early in 1900, they proved to be very strong engines taking 30 loaded coal wagons where the 0-6-0Ts could only manage 18 wagons unassisted.

After the GWR took over in 1908 they were rebuilt with Swindon taper boilers; unfortunately the firebox now sat on top of the bar frames which impaired their ability to work hard on the PTR without displacing the contents of the firebox.

Sharp Stewart received an order for three 0-8-2Ts similar to those supplied to the Barry Railway five years previously. Arriving in 1901 they differed slightly from their Barry Railway counterparts having a larger firebox, shorter boiler and various detail differences. With the arrival of these engines the PTR had sufficient large engines to work its main line trains without assistance.

The passenger traffic was fairly light with the exception of the colliery trains. In 1906 the PTR took delivery of a railmotor from Hawthorne Leslie, the only six-coupled railmotor to see service in Britain. It arrived in a livery of green lower panels and white upper panels; the engine unit was totally enclosed with side sheets, which caused many anxious moments for the footplate men as they battled up the gradients of the PTR in circumstances that O. Bulleid repeated nearly 50 years later when he built his 'Leader' class. The GWR replaced this railmotor with their own and sold it in 1920 to the Port of London Authority.

Suprisingly the PTR ordered eight bogie coaches from the Midland Carriage & Wagon Co. Originally they were two first/thirds, two thirds and four brake thirds. In 1904 provision

Above: No 26 on trip working at Port Talbot in 1910; the lamp irons have been altered to GWR pattern but no other alterations were carried out. Another similarity to Barry Railway practice can be seen in the brass numerals on the bunker backsheet. Sold out of service in 1934, No 26 was still going strong at Backworth Colliery up until 1967, and is now preserved on the Severn Valley Railway. *Courtesy A. Rees*

Below: GWR No 814, the former PTR No 27, at Port Talbot in 1926 with the abbreviated safety valve cover the GWR fitted to some of this class. The coal bunker was also rebuilt, but to no avail: by 1930 she had made her last trip to Swindon. *WRRC*

was made for second class passengers by converting two of the brake thirds into brake second/third composites. On the introduction of the railmotor in 1906, first class was abolished and the first/third composites became all thirds. The GWR abolished second class in 1911 and the bogie stock became four thirds and four brake thirds. For the colliers' trains the PTR purchased in 1899-1900 four second-hand coaches, two ex-GWR, the other pair ex-LNWR.

Passenger services began between Port Talbot and Blaengarw on 14 February 1898; the service was usually of four round trips a day with five on Saturdays. Additional trips were run between Port Talbot and Maesteg. None of the branches had a passenger service except for the colliers' trains that ran to the Mercentile Colliery on the former SWMR branch. Some PTR passenger trains started from the Aberavon station of the R&SBR. The GWR ran a Saturdays only train between Port Talbot and Tonmawr Junction from 1920 to 1930. Leaving Port Talbot at 9.00am and returning from Tonmawr at 3.40pm, it was probably the original skeleton service. Examination of large scale maps of the period reveal a small platform at Tonmawr, no building is evident.

The 1926 General Strike presaged the end of the PTR passenger trains; services were cut back to Maesteg from 12 September 1932 and completely withdrawn from 11 September 1933.

The goods stock reached 355 open wagons, 20 vans, 3 cattle wagons, 15 loco coal wagons and 14 goods brake vans. 204 of the open wagons were second-hand low sided wagons that were generally used internally within the docks. After the working agreement with the GWR commenced, the PTR retained control of the docks until the 1922 grouping; the goods stock was split between railway and docks, 240 wagons being allocated to the railway and 167 were docks wagons. Between 1908 and 1922 the GWR replaced some of the PTR wagon stock by second-hand wagons of its own, these being invariably older than the PTR wagons they nominally replaced.

The traffic of the PTR could be expressed in one word: 'coal'. In 1906 of a total of 1,195,560 tons carried, no less than 1,115,514 tons were coal class traffic; of this tonnage 853,665 tons were shipped through Port Talbot Docks.

Station buildings were neat little timber clap-boarded structures, of a standard pattern. The only differences were Port Talbot and Maesteg which were an enlarged version more in keeping with their requirements.

The PTR's signals were originally McKenzie Holland somersault pattern, though a lot of them were subsequently fitted with GWR finials and signal arms.

The end of the line for the PTR came on 9 May 1922 when it was absorbed by the GWR.

Left: Former PTR No 36 as GWR No 1326 built as a 2-4-0T by Sharp Stewart for the Barry Railway, the engine was rebuilt by the Barry as a 2-4-2T. It was sold to the PTR in 1898 and worked on passengers trains until the GWR takeover.
Courtesy C. W. Harris

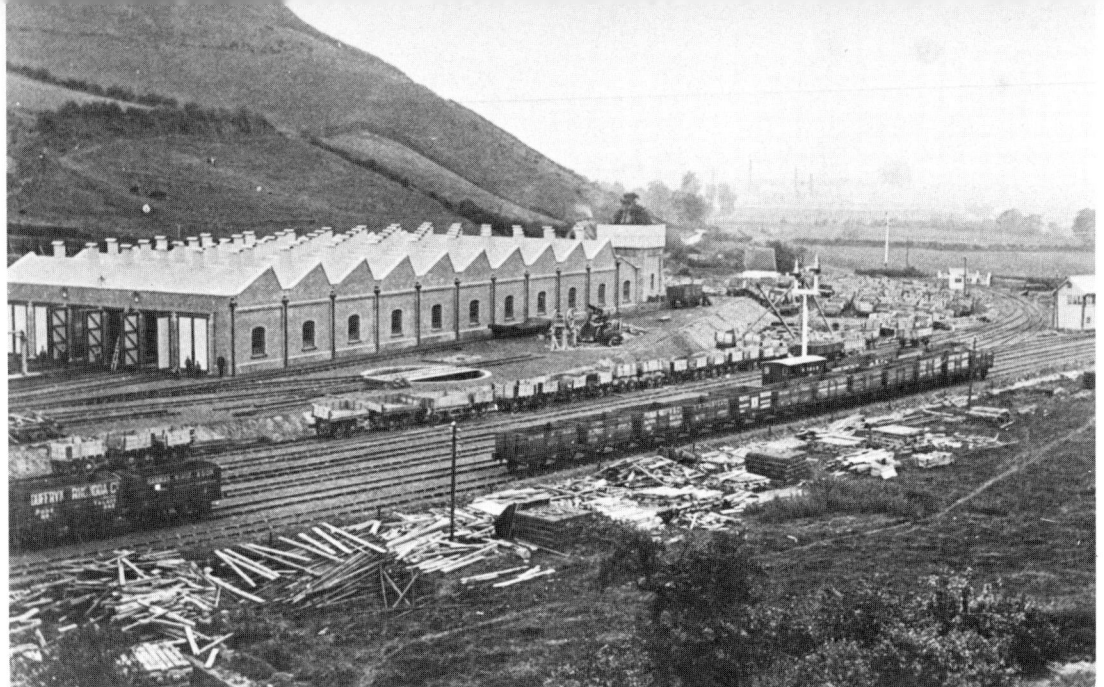

Above: Dyffryn yard, locomotive yard and workshops under construction in 1897 before the line was opened. The line of contractors' wagons are levelling the site where the coal stage was erected. The shed was closed in 1964 and its site is now a housing estate with no trace of its former use.
Courtesy South Glamorgan Libraries

Right: GWR No 959 — an 0-6-0ST of the 'Buffalo' class — on an engineers' train at Pontyrhyll. It is seen during construction of the junction and erection of station buildings preparatory to the PTR commencing to work up the Gawr Valley on 17 January 1898. *Courtesy R. Keene*

Below: Pontrhydyfen viaduct on the PTR mineral line which passed over the Afan Valley and heading for the Pelena Valley and the branches taken over from the SWMR. *Courtesy Afan Argoed Miners Museum*

The Rhondda & Swansea Bay Railway

There was considerable dissatisfaction with the services the GWR provided for Rhondda coal traffic to the Swansea Docks — it was not unknown for wagons to be over a week in transit. Swansea shipping and industrial magnates, therefore, called a public meeting in 1880 to estimate the measure of support they were likely to get in their attempts to develop Swansea into a major shipment port for Welsh steam coal. The ports of Cardiff and Newport had a virtual monopoly in this lucrative trade but Swansea, 40 miles nearer the Atlantic, was in an advantageous position to develop this proposed traffic provided that it could guarantee good transit times from the collieries to Swansea.

The measure of support for an independent railway was overwhelming and so the Rhondda & Swansea Bay Railway was born. Its proposed route was from Swansea Docks across the burrows to the Neath estuary, which it proposed to tunnel under, then run parallel to the South Wales line of the GWR past Briton Ferry, and then tunnel under Mynydd Gaer into the Afan Valley. From here it would take over the existing Cwmafan Mineral Railway, which had con-

nections to the docks at Briton Ferry and Port Talbot, run up the Afan Valley, tunnel through to the Rhondda and connect to the Taff Vale Railway at Treherbert.

The first act of Parliament, obtained in 1882, authorised construction between Aberavon and Cymmer. The Cwmafan Railway was realigned and relaid between Aberavon and Pontrhydyfen and was opened, with the new line to Cymmer in November 1885. The next section of the R&SBR to Blaengwynfi had to be built as a new railway running parallel to the upper section of the GWR's Llynfi and Ogmore branch because of the intransigent and antagonistic attitude that the GWR displayed towards the R&SBR. The great 3,463yd long tunnel beneath Mynydd Blaenrhondda was opened in July 1890 with only five fatalities among the contractor's workforce. This upper section of the R&SBR — with the longest railway tunnel in Wales — cost £250,000. Passenger trains started working through to Treherbert on 14 March 1895.

The original powers to construct a railway between Aberavon and Swansea were allowed to lapse, as it was proposed to use the GWR

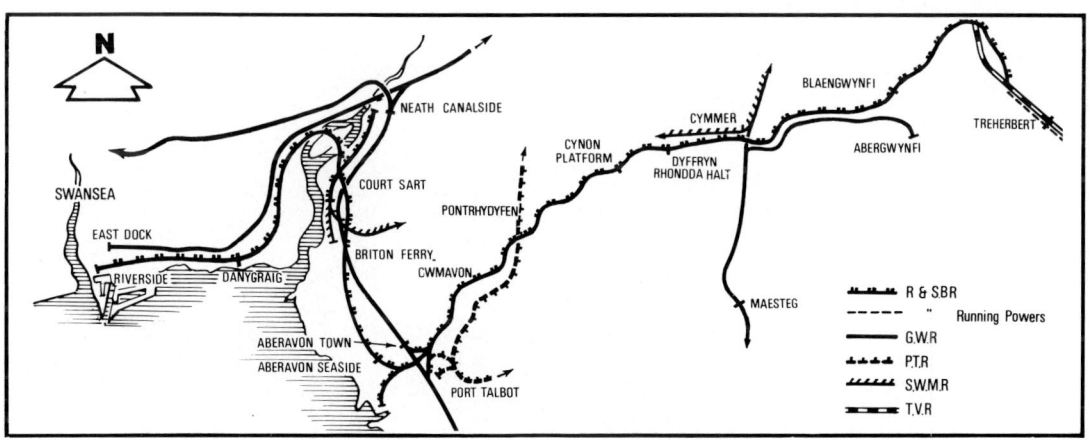

Right: In 1885 the R&SBR
ordered its first 0-6-2T's from
Kitson's. The engines were
practically identical to the
TVR 'M' class. Subsequently
the R&SBR amended the
design to suit its
requirements. The amended
0-6-2T, with its longer firebox
and smaller boiler, became
the backbone of the R&SBR
locomotive department.
Though primarily mineral
engines, they were often
pressed into passenger
service when required. Here is
No 16 in original condition
standing on the level crossing
at Cymmer.
Courtesy A. Rees

Centre right: No 21, built by
Kitson's in 1899, on
passenger duties at Swansea
Riverside in 1907. The GWR
takeover of the R&SBR was
making its mark on the
locomotives, by now; No 21
had acquired a GWR toolbox
and the safety valves had
been encased in an elongated
version of their bonnet.
WRRC

Bottom right: The three
2-4-2Ts were, except for their
wheel arrangement,
practically identical to the
0-6-2Ts. The former R&SBR
No 19 was rebuilt at Swindon
in 1921 with a taper boiler
and standard cab, also with a
peculiar sloping extension to
the coal bunker. Afterwards
No 19 was sent to Barry to
work passenger trains, but
was not liked by her crews
and was reduced to goods
trips. As GWR No 1310, seen
here, the engine was reduced
to menial duties at Barry in
1923 and she was withdrawn
in 1930. *WRRC*

between these two points. Again the GWR displayed their usual tactics towards the R&SBR — their ideas about connecting junctions were totally inadequate for the existing traffic let alone the anticipated increase. An alternative act was hurriedly obtained in 1891 for a new railway to Briton Ferry, with a branch line from Court Sart to Neath. The River Neath was now to be crossed by a curved swing bridge, after which the railway was to be routed across the Burrows to Swansea. The opening to Briton Ferry for mineral traffic took place on 30 December 1893, a year later coal was running through to Swansea Docks. The Neath branch and passenger trains to Danygraig both opened together on 14 March 1895. This section of the R&SBR was built for £20,000 per mile compared with the £38,000 per mile the rest of the R&SBR had cost. The final section to the passenger terminus at Swansea Riverside was opened on 7 May 1895. Unlike most railways primarily promoted for the shipment of coal, the R&SBR owned no docks at all, though it had its own coal hoists at the King's and the Prince of Wales docks in Swansea.

A Neath, Pontardawe & Brynamman Railway was incorporated by an act of 1895. It proposed to connect the GWR's Brynamman branch with a railway running down the Clydach Valley, connecting with the Midland Railway at Pontardawe and finally connecting with the Vale of Neath and the South Wales main line of the GWR. But no construction ever took place. Then, despite fierce GWR opposition, the Act was revived in 1902 with additional powers to connect with the

R&SBR and the Barry Railway was given powers to subscribe to the NP&BR.

The prospect for the GWR was to say the least very unpalatable. The Barry Railway was poised to expand westward from Coity Junction, Bridgend, by means of running powers over the PTR and the R&SBR that it was actively negotiating, and it was in the position to tap the Ogmore, Llynfi, Afan and Clydach valleys. Belatedly the GWR made concessions to the Swansea shipping and industrial interests. Additionally the company started to make friendly overtures towards the R&SBR, culminating in a proposal that they should work the R&SBR and guarantee an increasing dividend to the shareholders.

As colliery developments in the Afan valley had not been as rapid as the promotors of the R&SBR had desired, and the Parliamentary and constructional costs had been much higher than anticipated, the returns to the shareholders had been very small, though the position was quietly improving. A dividend of $\frac{3}{4}$% in 1897 had risen to $1\frac{1}{2}$% in 1902 and the position was improving. But the GWR offer was of a guaranteed 5% for the Preference shareholders, while the Ordinary shareholders were to receive an immediate 3% rising to 4% in 1907, and from 1908 they were to receive 5%. On the recommendation of the directors these terms were accepted, and the GWR's lease of the R&SBR took effect from 1 July 1906.

The early locomotives of the R&SBR included two oddities; the first, No 2 an ex-LNWR 0-6-0

Left: An up R&SBR passenger train composed of TVR coaches working through from Swansea to Cardiff, arriving at Blaenrhandda station at the turn of the century behind one of the 2-4-2Ts.
Courtesy C. Batstone

93

Right: Blaencwm signalbox at the end of the double line from Treherbert; this controlled entrance to the Rhondda Tunnel which burrowed beneath Mynydd Blaenrhondda to give access to the Afan Valley. *Courtesy C. Batstone*

Below: The Western portal of the Rhondda Tunnel above Blaengwynfi had an inscribed commemorative stone placed above the key stone of the arch. When the tunnel entrance was closed and the surrounding area landscaped following closure, this stone was retrieved and is now on display at the Afan Argoed Miners Museum.
Courtesy Afan Argoed Miners Museum

Below right: Blaengwynfi station in about 1900 with staff and one of the 0-6-2Ts. Though the R&SBR locomotives were black they were always gleaming.
Courtesy Afan Argoed Miners Museum

tender engine latterly numbered 1882 by that company, was purchased in 1884. It was sold to William Westlake (a contractor in Swansea Docks) in 1891. The second odd man was an 0-6-0ST purchased from the contractors Lucas & Aird, who had numbered it No 131. Known as *Lucas* or 131 it was used as a ballast engine and, after being out of use for some years, was sold in 1905. A poor photograph of *Lucas* suggests that it could have been a Kitson production.

The first new engines the R&SBR purchased were a pair of 0-6-0STs built by Beyer Peacock, delivered in 1885-6: another three were delivered in 1889. They were intended for shunting and trip workings. After the grouping the GWR sold two of them to colliery companies; the last of them, old R&SBR No 5, was scrapped by the NCB in 1956.

The first 0-6-2T arrived in 1886: it was practical identically to the TVR 'M' class that had just preceded it. Like the TVR, the R&SBR soon decided that the 0-6-2T was the answer to

its problems. A further 12 were delivered between 1889 and 1899, modified with a larger firebox and a shorter boiler barrel. Reboilered by the GWR, they were withdrawn between 1926 and 1936.

In 1895 Kitson's delivered three 2-4-2Ts for the passenger services. Except for the altered wheel arrangement they were practically identical to the 0-6-2Ts. No 19 was drastically rebuilt at Swindon in 1922 and was sent to Barry fitted with a Swindon tapered boiler and cab, and a peculiar extension to the coal bunker that made it look like a coal scuttle. The engine proved to be very unpopular because of its poor steaming abilities and it was reduced to shunting duties. It was withdrawn in 1928 as the last of its class, a very short life after such an extensive rebuild.

In 1901 two 0-6-2Ts were purchased from the PTR; less than four years old they were very similar to the R&SBR 0-6-2Ts. Little altered by the GWR they were withdrawn in 1928-9.

Finally by 1904 four enlarged 0-6-2Ts with

4ft 9in coupled wheels and a larger boiler had arrived. They proved to be the last locomotives the R&SBR ordered. They were not rebuilt by the GWR and were withdrawn as they were stopped for heavy repairs between 1927 and 1936.

After the working agreement of 1906 the GWR drafted in various standard classes of their own, three '45xx' class 2-6-2Ts taking over many of the passenger duties. Soon after they commenced working the R&SBR services, a letter arrived at Paddington from the Taff Vale Railway drawing the GWR's attention the to fact that the concession to work into Treherbert was granted by Parliament to the R&SBR only, not to the GWR, and that the latter should desist forthwith. The GWR hurriedly fitted R&SBR numberplates to all the GWR engines and renumbered coaches that they had drafted in.

Passenger services commenced with a dozen six-wheeled coaches purchased between 1885 and 1889 from Brown Marshall, fitted with the Westinghouse brake which had to be converted to vacuum brake before through workings to the TVR commenced. At the same time additional coaches were delivered as the R&SBR services were transformed into a direct Swansea-Treherbert link to the TVR. By 1894, 34 additional six-wheeled coaches were in use and a

year later 26 41ft 0in bogie coaches arrived from the Ashbury Carriage & Wagon Co. In 1905 nine ex-Mersey Railway four-wheeled coaches were purchased.

The R&SBR passenger services were usually seven trains a day either way between Swansea and Treherbert with extras on Saturdays, with a Sunday service of two either way. On weekdays six trains worked through to Pontypridd, Cardiff and Penarth on the TVR, likewise the corresponding TVR sets worked through to Swansea (Riverside). This through working was confined to the coach sets, both companies always changing engines at Treherbert.

The usual make up of a R&SBR passenger train was a workmen's coach immediately behind the engine followed by a brake van, a third (an extra third on Mondays and Saturdays), a first/second composite coach, a third and a brake third.

Below left: The rival establishment on the opposite side of the narrow valley was called Abergwynfi, the terminus of the GWR passenger service up the Llynfi Valley. Here is the old signalbox and gang of platelayers in 1916. Beyond the station the track continued as a mineral line to collieries sunk by Sir Daniel Gooch and others.
Courtesy Afan Argoed Miners Museum

Bottom left: The R&SBR station at Cymmer, a temporary terminus for passenger trains for the period 1885-90 after which it was opened for the extension to Blaengwynfi. Now all of it has been demolished except for the refreshment rooms on the left that are still open for business.
Courtesy Afan Argoed Miners Museum

Below: A photograph of Cymmer Afan, as the R&SBR station was called from 1924, with passengers waiting for a Aberavon seaside excursion. Behind the platform is a colliers' train, in the background is a train drawn up in Cymmer General station en route for Maesteg and Bridgend. The close proximity of the two railways illustrates the folly of rival companies in such a narrow valley.
Courtesy Afan Argoed Miners Museum

The GWR did not alter the basic R&SBR services except to withdraw the Sunday service during the early 1920s. When Swansea (Riverside) was closed in 1933, services were diverted to East Dock station until that station was closed in 1935 when services were diverted to the High Street station.

In 1920 an interesting summer working commenced, starting from the Rhymney Railways Parade station in Cardiff running via Caerphilly and the PC&NR to Pontypridd, by the TVR to Treherbert and by the R&SBR to Briton Ferry, where the Swansea avoiding line of the GWR was gained, from here calling at Llanelly and Carmarthen. Then it headed north over the single lines of the former Carmarthen & Cardigan and M&M railways to Aberystwyth. GWR coaches were used throughout and this working survived until it was withdrawn after nationalisation.

The goods stock numbered only 93 wagons at the end of 1898, but once the Rhondda Tunnel was opened with its own route to Swansea, a large number of additional wagons were delivered from various makers. By 1906 the R&SBR owned 234 vans (these would be required for the large consignments of flour dispatched from Weaver's Mill, Swansea to the Rhondda), 307 open wagons, 12 timber trucks, 4 cattle wagons, 15 loco coal wagons, 245 mineral wagons (used for the copper and iron ingot traffic), 20 ballast wagons, 16 goods brake vans, 2 pilot vans and a breakdown crane. Some of the original wagons had been withdrawn and replacements built at Danygraig Workshops. The GWR subsequently provided replacement stock from its own, usually older than the original R&SBR stock it replaced.

Danygraig Workshops, opened in 1896, was fully equipped to carry out heavy locomotive repairs, and, with the adjacent carriage and wagon shops, was a considerable investment. In the GWR's hands, however, it was never to achieve its true potential.

The signalling equipment supplied to the R&SBR was the normal well proven McKenzie & Holland somersault patent. Again the GWR fitted its own replacement signals to the original posts giving a peculiar appearance to these renewals.

On 9 May 1922 the R&SBR was absorbed by the GWR; though it never achieved its fullest expectations as a railway, it certainly proved to be a good investment for the shareholders. The only loser was the GWR, which had to guarantee the dividends.

Left: A period notice preserved in the Afan Argoed Miners Museum commemorates the opening of the R&SBR to Cymmer on 2 November 1885. *Courtesy Afan Argoed Miners Museum.*

Below: McKenzie Holland somersault signals at Aberavon seaside station. The GWR soon substituted their own signal arms on the original posts. *G. H. W. Clifford courtesy C. C. Green*

RHONDDA & SWANSEA BAY
RAILWAY.

THE SECOND SECTION
Of the Rhondda & Swansea Bay Railway, from

PONTRHYDYFEN TO CYMMER
WILL BE

OPENED
FOR PASSENGER AND MINERAL TRAFFIC

ON MONDAY NEXT,
THE 2nd DAY OF NOVEMBER.

Passenger Trains Will run as follow until further notice:—

WEEK DAYS ONLY.

UP TRAINS.

	a.m.	p.m.	p.m.
ABERAVON Dep.	7.55	1.10	5.30
CWMAVON	8.1	1.16	5.36
PONTRHYDYFEN	8.9	1.24	5.44
CYMMER Arr.	8.21	1.36	5.56

DOWN TRAINS.

	a.m.	p.m.	p.m.
CYMMER Dep.	8.30	1.45	6.5
PONTRHYDYFEN	8.43	1.58	6.18
CWMAVON	8.51	2.6	6.26
ABERAVON Arr.	8.57	2.12	6.32

For further information apply to Mr JOHN DAVID Superintendent of Traffic Cwmavon

H. S. LUDLOW, Secretary.

The Rhymney Railway

Promoted by the Trustees of the Bute Estates who had acquired valuable mineral rights in the Rhymney Valley, the Rhymney Raiway was incorporated by an Act of Parliament dated 14 July 1854, to build a railway between the Rhymney Iron Works and Hengoed where a junction was to be made with the Newport, Abergavenny & Hereford Railway. A proposed line to the Taff Vale Railway, at Llancaiach was defeated. An amended act of 2 July 1855 authorised an extension to join the TVR at Taffs Well, also a line from Corckherbtown Cardiff to the Bute East Dock with running powers over the TVR between these points. The Docks branch was the first section of Rhymney Railway to be opened in September 1857. The main line to Rhymney opened for goods trains on 25 February 1858, passenger trains commenced running on 31 March 1858.

The early years were very difficult: traffic was slow to develop, disputes with the TVR soon arose — principally because the Rhymney Railway had free transhipping facilities at the East Dock while the TVR had to pay heavily for

Below: The Rhymney Railway started life in 1857 with six 0-6-0 tender engines built by Vulcan Foundry. Quite large for the time, they were classified 'A' by C. T. Hurry Riches on his appointment as Locomotive Superintendent of the Rhymney Railway in 1906, but he withdrew these old warriors before the end of 1908. Here is one of them just before the end, on a passenger train at Merthyr. Nos 4 and 5 were both stationed at Merthyr for working the GWR-RR joint line.
R. E. Thomas courtesy C. C. Green

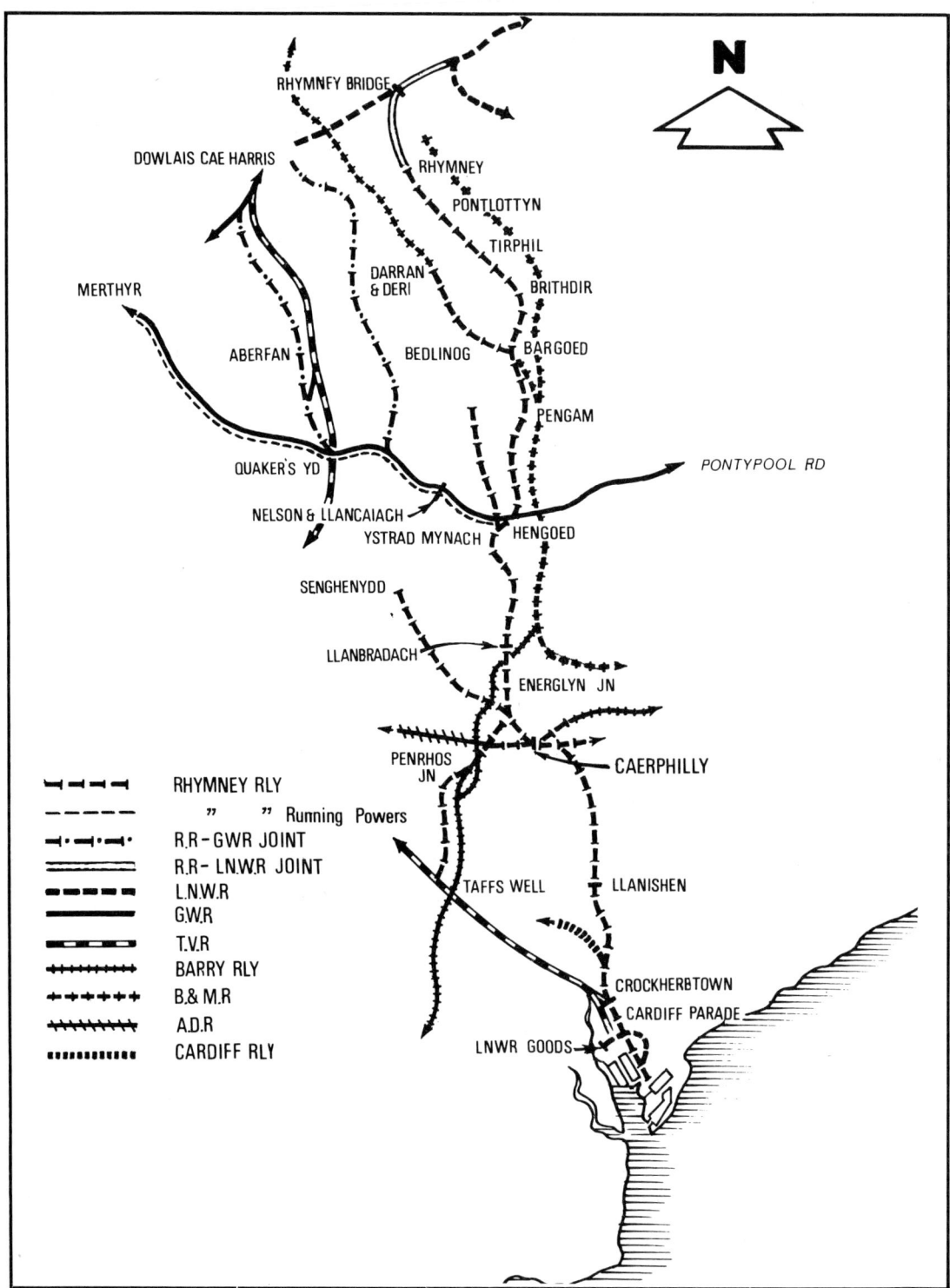

N

RHYMNEY BRIDGE

DOWLAIS CAE HARRIS

RHYMNEY

PONTLOTTYN

TIRPHIL

MERTHYR

DARRAN & DERI

BRITHDIR

ABERFAN

BEDLINOG

BARGOED

PENGAM

QUAKER'S YD

PONTYPOOL RD

NELSON & LLANCAIACH

YSTRAD MYNACH

HENGOED

SENGHENYDD

LLANBRADACH

ENERGLYN JN

PENRHOS JN

CAERPHILLY

TAFFS WELL

LLANISHEN

CROCKHERBTOWN

CARDIFF PARADE

LNWR GOODS

┣╍╍╍╍┫	RHYMNEY RLY
– – – –	” ” Running Powers
╍·╍·╍·╍·	R.R – GWR JOINT
═══════	R.R – L.N.W.R JOINT
▬ ▬ ▬ ▬	L.N.W.R
▬▬▬▬▬▬	G.W.R
▬▬ ▬▬	T.V.R
+++++++	BARRY RLY
++++++	B.& M.R
✕✕✕✕✕✕	A.D.R
▪▪▪▪▪▪▪	CARDIFF RLY

98

similar facilities at the West Dock. In 1860 the Bute Estates promoted a bill to lease the Rhymney Railway but were heavily defeated in Parliament. The next year the Rhymney Railway attempted to promote its own line between Taffs Well and Cardiff which incurred TVR opposition and counter-proposals that were successful.

By 1861 traffic was rising and agreement was reached with the Bute Estates to capitalise the arrears of rent and dock dues.

At last on 25 July 1864, the Rhymney Railway obtained its act to build a new line between Caerphilly and Cardiff. The TVR's opposition was bought off by the Bute Estates allowing it access to the west side of the East Dock; the Rhymney Railway also agreed to continue to haul its Penarth traffic over the TVR.

Through the 1860s during a time of financial crisis and general uncertainty, the Rhymney struggled to construct its new line, with the tunnel under Caerphilly Common. This proved to be a source of additional expense, but finally the line was opened on 1 April 1871.

Relations with the Brecon & Merthyr Railway had been friendly until that company began to promote lines that conflicted with the interests of the Rhymney. Having purchased the old 'Rumney Tramroad' in 1863 the B&MR now obtained an act to construct a railway down the Bargoed Rhymney Valley over the very route of the Rhymney Railway's authorised line by its revised act. The many restrictive clauses in the two companies' acts forced them to compromise in the end. The Rhymney Railway built the railway between Bargoed and Deri Junction while the B&MR built the remainder. The Rhymney Railway was to have running powers over the B&MR to the collieries at Fochriw, while the B&MR was to have unrestricted passage for its through traffic. The B&MR's attempt to promote its own line to Cardiff was bought off with running powers from Caerphilly to Taffs Well and Cardiff (Rhymney); these powers were never exercised.

The Rhymney opened its line to Deri Junction in March 1864, but the B&MR could not make use of it till they had completed their original line to Merthyr. New and powerful allies for the Rhymney began to appear — first, the LNWR which leased the Merthyr, Tredegar & Abergavenny Railway during its construction of 1862. Wanting access to Cardiff, the LNWR now promoted a joint line with the Rhymney between Nant y Bwlch and Rhymney, with running powers over each other's railways. These powers the Rhymney Railway did not exercise, but the LNWR from the opening of the joint line on 2 October 1871, began to run goods trains through to Cardiff. This meant that the LNWR no longer had to make the journey to Cardiff via Newport with the transhipping to the broad gauge which the previous arrangement had necessitated.

In 1867, the Rhymney Railway promoted a joint line with the GWR up the Taff Bargoed Valley to Dowlais. As the GWR had absorbed the West Midland Railway, the Rhymney built a connecting line between Ystrad Mynach and Penallta Junction which opened on 27 September 1871, with the additional bonus of running powers granted by the GWR to Hirwain where the Bute Estates had collieries. With the Dowlais traffic that it gained, the Rhymney had certainly

Left: The Rhymney Railway, at the wishes of its General Manager Cornelius Lundie who took overall responsibility for every department of the Company, settled upon double-framed saddle tank engines that were to fulfil the Rhymney need till the early 1900s. The first class was the '23-44' afterwards Class I. No 33 of this class was built in 1874 and, after reboilering and fitting with a full cab and Westinghouse brake, was placed on the Duplicate List as No 033 in 1920. Renumbered No 659 by the GWR the engine was the oldest on the Rhymney at grouping. Here it is, still earning its keep in Cardiff Docks in 1924 — it was withdrawn the following year as the last of the class. *WRRC*

turned the tables on the TVR. The opening of the Taff Bargoed line through to Dowlais (Caer Harris) in 1876 caused enough extra traffic to make the doubling of the line below Ystrad Mynach essential. It also made more locomotives and wagons desperately needed. All this expenditure depressed dividends until 1875, after which the fortunes of the Rhymney were definitely on the upturn.

A further joint line with the GWR Quaker's Yard & Merthyr Joint Line — was opened on 1 April 1886. This again penetrated to the very roots of the TVR, and enabled the Rhymney Railway to gain access to collieries in the Merthyr Vale.

The Pontypridd, Caerphilly & Newport Railway opened between Pontypridd TVR and Penrhos Junction, Caerphilly in 1884 had running powers over the Rhymney, through Caerphilly to gain access to the B&MR's mineral branch from Machen. Though it gave the Rhymney direct access to Pontypridd, the TVR successfully prevented all attempts to route Rhymney traffic over the PC&NR.

An act to build a railway between Caerphilly and Nine Mile Point on the Sirhowy line of the LNWR was obtained in 1888. This would have given the Sirhowy Valley collieries direct access to Cardiff; but it was never constructed as the GWR paid the Rhymney £10,000 a year for 10 years to abandon the project.

The small branch line from Aber Junction to Senghenydd opened on 1 February 1894; promoted to serve colliery developments it had a frequent passenger service. The Cylla branch opened between 1906 and 1909 running northwards for two miles from Ystrad Mynach as a mineral line only.

A most damaging penetration of the Rhymney's system occurred when the Barry Railway spread its tentacles, first obtaining access via the TVR at Taffs Well with running powers to Caerphilly on 5 August 1891. This initial penetration did not satisfy the Barry Railway for long and it promoted its own line from Tynycaeau to Penrhos, again with running powers into Caerphilly. This was opened on 1 August 1901. A further extension of this line from Penrhos Lower Junction to reach the B&MR and penetrate to Rhymney over that railway was opened on 2 January 1905. Within two years

1,000,000 tons of Rhymney Valley coal was wending its way annually to Barry Docks.

Finally an old ally in an entirely new guise, the Bute Dock Co tried to spread into Rhymney territory by its act of 1897, under which it became the Cardiff Railway. Initially it proposed amalgamating with the Rhymney but this, with the majority of the proposed extensions to its system, was defeated — except for its new line from Pontypridd to Heath Junction with running powers over the Rhymney to Cardiff, which in the event proved to be only a minor irritation.

The 1909-10 amalgamation of the Rhymney, TVR and Cardiff Railways which proposed to fuse their railways and dock interests into one unified system was defeated by the strong opposition of the Barry and ADR and the reluctance of the governments of the day to the creation of monopolies. In 1917 A. E. Prosser, the General Manager of the Rhymney Railway, undertook the additional duties of managing the TVR and Cardiff Railway and this temporary arrangement lasted till the grouping.

The first locomotives that the Rhymney acquired were six 0-6-0 tender engines built by Vulcan Foundry in 1857. With their 4ft 9in wheels they were equally at home on passenger trains; in fact, when they were displaced by later engines because of the strain of the heavier mineral trains, they were fitted with the Westinghouse brake and finished their days on lighter passenger and workmen's trains. The first passenger engines arrived in 1858 — three 2-4-0 engines also by the Vulcan Foundry followed by another one in 1861. The original trio were rebuilt as saddle tank engines and were withdrawn in 1895; the 1861 engine was rebuilt as a side tank engine and lasted till 1906.

Also in 1858 two long-boilered 0-6-0STs for shunting duties arrived from Vulcan Foundry. Afterwards rebuilt and fitted with cabs, they were withdrawn in 1910-11.

In 1859 Kitson's supplied four small outside-framed 0-6-0 tender engines; one was rebuilt as a saddle tank, the other three were fitted with the Eames steam brake, to which the Rhymney and the B&MR gave extensive trials lasting many years. The last of these engines was withdrawn in 1917.

The final tender engines ordered were four 0-6-0s delivered from Kitson's in 1867-8. Also fitted with the Eames brake and cabs when reboiled, three were withdrawn in 1912 and the withdrawal of No 022 during 1915 saw the end of tender engines on the Rhymney.

As the financial position of the Rhymney improved, the first engines designed by the General Manager, Cornelius Lundie (who had overall responsibility for all departments), were supplied by Sharp Stewart in 1872. The first was a batch of a class of double framed 0-6-0 saddle tanks; further batches of these locomotives arrived in 1874-78, and they eventually totally 22. With brass numerals on the chimneys, bunker back plates and other distinctive features, they were more suitable for the expanding heavy coal

and mineral traffic. Though originally only fitted with a hand brake, all were reboiled by 1902 when most of them were fitted with Westinghouse brakes, the remainder being fitted with the Eames brake. C. T. Hurry Riches fitted them with his standard saddle tank boiler and cut back the rear sheets of the cab to give a separate coal bunker unlike the original allover cab. The first withdrawall were in 1914 but World War 1 gave the remainder an extended life, three being sold to the War Department in 1916. The remainder were withdrawn in 1920-21 except for Nos 033 and 036 which survived till 1925.

As Cornelius Lundie was satisfied with the performance of his saddle tanks, 12 improved

Left: Having found a good strong design of locomotive that suited its conditions (and met the requirements of Mr Lundie — perhaps a more important consideration!), the next development was an enlargement to 0-6-2ST of the '57' class built between 1890-1900. This class always did a fair amount of passenger work — as exemplified by No 83 in 1905 at Merthyr. The Rhymney was the only Welsh railway to standardise on the Westinghouse brake, much to the annoyance of its neighbours. *Courtesy C. C. Green*

Below: A strange fact is that the two engines of the 'L' class that remained as 2-4-2STs to the end, were the last survivors of the class. Former Rhymney No 65 is seen as GWR 1324 at Cardiff Docks in 1924 on the Caerphilly works train. Nos 1324, 1325 were withdrawn in 1928. *WRRC*

locomotives of the same type were delivered in 1884 fitted with a better cab with side sheets and a separate coal bunker. These were afterwards fitted with vacuum, Westinghouse and Eames brakes — rebuilding commenced in 1901. C. T. Hurry Riches rebuilt more of them with his saddle tank boiler and classified them as Class J. He also replaced the Eames brake with steam brakes on those engines that had this fitting. Withdrawal commenced in 1921, with most withdrawn soon after the grouping, the last survivor being sold to the Ocean Coal Co in 1927.

The next development was the '57' class — an 0-6-2ST enlargement of the previous '45' class. The first batch arrived in 1890 from the Vulcan Foundry; additional engines were ordered until they formed a class of 47 engines in 1900. Most of the later engines were built with Westinghouse or vacuum brakes for passenger train operations. The purely goods engines were fitted with the Eames brake. Rebuilding commenced in 1902,

and the rebuilt locomotives were classified 'K' and were fitted with C. T. Hurry Riches standard saddle tank boilers from 1908; this same boiler was fitted to the '23-45' and 'J' class locomotives No 97 achieved immortality in 1909 when it blew up because the cow tail lever on the Ramsbottom safety valve had been assembled upside down the prevented the boiler 'blowing off'. The explosion tore the engine apart, killing three men who were trying to discover what was wrong with it. After this C. T. Hurry Riches had Ross pop valves fitted to all new boilers. The rest of the class was still active at grouping, but the GWR removed the Westinghouse brakes and replaced them with vacuum brakes. Five of the class were rebuilt with pannier tanks, which never seemed to fit in with their double-framed rugged character and — what was more important — reduced their water capacity. The last saddle tanks were withdrawn in 1931, the pannier tank rebuilds soon followed them and all were gone by 1934.

Above: Former Rhymney Railway No 95 seen as GWR No 138 at Cardiff Docks shed in 1924, very little altered except for the substitution of a vacuum pump for the former Westinghouse equipment. However in 1926 No 138 was fitted with pannier tanks which did nothing for its looks. The engine was withdrawn in 1934. *WRRC*

The final form of double-framed saddle tanks was the '62-66' class, a 2-4-2ST introduced in 1890 as replacements for the old 2-4-0T rebuilds, classified as 'L' in 1906. Number 62 and 63 were converted to 0-6-2STs in 1908 when they were reboilered, afterwards they took over the Cardiff-Merthyr workings. No 64 additionally was rebuilt as an 0-6-2ST in 1911, and after 1915 Nos 65 and 66 were fitted for auto-train working. No 62 was withdrawn in 1921 leaving two 0-6-2STs and two 2-4-2STs to be handed over to the GWR at grouping. Nos 63 and 64 were soon withdrawn leaving Nos 65 and 66 still with their original wheel arrangement, these locomotives survived till 1928.

At the end of his long reign Cornelius Lundie and his Locomotive Superintendent R. Evans ordered the first modern 0-6-2 side tank engines. Fitted with Belpaire boilers these six engines were not entirely successful as built, because the steaming qualities of the boilers were not as good

as desired. In fact it was one of the problems that C. T. Hurry Riches had to resolve when he took up the position of Locomotive Superintendent of the Rhymney in 1906. Classified 'M', one was reboilered with a round-topped boiler in 1910, and from 1916 they were reboilered with the 'R' class boiler which greatly improved their capabilities. Two were withdrawn by the GWR before World War 2, the last survivor being condemned in 1951.

The first class C. T. Hurry Riches designed was his 'R' class of 1907. Five were delivered in 1907-9, while a further 10 were delivered in 1921 as replacements to older engines. After the grouping the GWR rebuilt five of them with taper boilers, but the last survivors were old Nos 36 and 38 still with Rhymney boilers. They had the unhappy distinction of being the last Rhymney Railway locomotives in service when they were withdrawn in 1957.

As replacement shunting engines four 0-6-0Ts

Left: In 1903 the Rhymney ordered its first modern 0-6-2Ts. How much of the design was the work of R. Jenkins the Loco Superintendent, or of Mr Lundie, who did not retire till 1908 just before his 90th birthday, is not clear. However C. T. Hurry Riches who was appointed to the position of Locomotive Superintendent of the Rhymney at the beginning of 1906 soon established his own standards. His first class of engine, the 'Rs' built in 1907 and 1909, were intended for heavy mineral trains; a further batch was delivered in 1921. The last one them, No 62 is seen with its solid Rhymney Railway features unaltered, on the former TVR shed at Cathays in 1927. *WRRC*

Below: C. T. Hurry Riches built a class of three passenger engines in 1909, and a modified engine classed as 'P1' followed in 1917. This engine, No 31, is on Cardiff Docks shed in 1923 still in mint Rhymney condition with the simplified livery. *WRRC*

Right: The first three engines of the new 'A1' class were delivered in 1914; five others ordered then were not delivered till 1918. Here is No 24 of 1914 with crew and staff in 1920; No 24 retained a Rhymney boiler to the end of its days in 1950. *WRRC*

were obtained from Hudswell Clarke in 1908; classified as 'S' they took over the heavy shunting in Cardiff Docks. Three further engines arrived in 1919. Fitted with Westinghouse brakes they were classified as 'S1'. The GWR rebuilt the original quartet with taper boilers and they all were taken out of service during 1953-4.

The first Hurry Riches passenger engines were the three engines of the 'P' class — a 5ft 0in coupled wheeled version of the earlier 0-6-2Ts. No 5 was rebuilt with a Belpaire boiler in 1915. A further engine was delivered new in 1917 and was classified as 'P1'. The GWR rebuilt these locomotives with taper boilers after which they survived World War 2, the last one being withdrawn in 1955.

A goods version of the 'P' class appeared in 1910, the Class A. The first batch of 10 engines and another six delivered the next year were replacements for old saddle tank engines. In 1913 further engines arrived fitted with Belpaire boilers; these were classified 'A1'. Replacement Belpaire boilers were obtained and fitted to some of the original 'As'. The final additions to the class arrived in 1918. After the grouping the GWR reversed the process and 'A1s' were fitted with the repaired round top boilers of the 'As'. Other engines were rebuilt with taper boilers. The whole class remained complete till 1948 when withdrawal started. This process was fairly rapid and all were gone by 1955.

The final passenger engines of the Rhymney Railway were the four engines of the 'AP' class delivered in 1921 from Hudswell Clarke. Fitted again with 5ft 0in coupled wheels they were kept in immaculate condition during their brief Rhymney careers. The GWR rebuilt two of them

with taper boilers during 1928-9, the other pair retained their Rhymney boilers till 1949. During 1954-5 they were all withdrawn from the lowly shunting duties they had been reduced to.

C. T. Hurry Riches followed the lead of his father on the TVR and introduced two railmotors in 1907. The engine units were built by Hudswell Clarke while the coachwork was supplied by Cravens Ltd. As originally built there was considerable vibration between the engine units and the coach portions. This fault was overcome by rebuilding the engine units as 0-4-2s with an extension frame to carry the leading end of the coach body. After this they returned to duty, one railmotor running usually between Senghenydd and Caerphilly with an occasional trip along the B&MR's Machen branch. The other unit was based at Rhymney and worked to Ystrad Mynach and over the Merthyr joint line. This latter service was not really suitable for a railmotor with its limited accommodation, so railmotor No 2 was withdrawn in 1910. The coach portion was rebuilt into a brake third while the engine unit was rebuilt as an 0-6-0T with a water tank and a coal bunker built on to the rear of the engine unit. Numbered 120 this engine took up duties as the Caerphilly Yard pilot. Railmotor No 1 continued on the Senghenydd branch until 1919 when it to went into the works and after similar treatment the engine unit emerged as 0-6-0T No 121. The coach portion was again rebuilt as a brake third. Nos 120 and 121 did not last long after the grouping, both being withdrawn in 1925.

The Rhymney Railway commenced its passenger services in 1858 with a few four-wheeled coaches supplied by C. Williams and the Railway

Wagon Co of Oldbury. In fact two first class coaches supplied by the latter manufacturer were part of the Caerphilly Works train till 1912. The carriage and wagon shop in Cardiff Docks began constructing six-wheeled coaches during the 1880s. After the carriage shop was opened in the new Caerphilly Works a lot more replacement coaches were constructed leading to the building of bogie coaches in 1914. A final batch of bogie coaches was supplied by the Gloucester Carriage & Wagon Co in 1920. The majority of the bogie coaches was fitted with wooden slatted seats, and discerning passengers preferred the older six-wheeled stock with its upholstered seats.

The Rhymney Railway occasionally ventured into the second-hand market: in 1909 12 LSWR six-wheeled thirds were purchased and fitted with Westinghouse brakes. In 1912 a further 19 LSWR carriages arrived. Finally, in 1914, 12 coaches were purchased from the Metropolitan District Railway. All these second-hand coaches were used as workmen's coaches. After World War 1 the Rhymney began to fit its engines and coaches for steam heating but half the stock was still dependent on the old foot warmers at group-

Top: The first of the A class, No 14 of 1910, was rebuilt with a taper boiler at Swindon in 1933. It is seen here at Barry in 1938 as GWR No 56, the engine was to serve through another world war before withdrawal in 1953. *WRRC*

Below: 'AP' class No 37 dwarfs the mixed collection of six-wheeled coaches comprising its train. It was fitted with steam heating pipes from new as the Rhymney Railway belatedly decided to dispense with the foot warmers that used to be placed in the compartments in cold weather.
G. H. W. Clifford courtesy C. C. Green

Above: C. T. Hurry Riches' final passenger engines were the four 'AP' class locomotives delivered in 1921. They were the final development of Rhymney Railway locomotive practice. The second engine, No 36, was soon at work on the Cardiff-Rhymney main line trains.
G. H. W. Clifford courtesy C. C. Green

ing. By adopting the Westinghouse brakes, the Rhymney Railway created problems for the surrounding railways obliging them to supply dual-braked stock on through workings, because the few vacuum-braked coaches that the Rhymney possessed were unsuitable for such workings. Through foreign vacuum-braked trains were handled by the handful of 0-6-2STs that were fitted with vacuum brakes. By arrangement with the Barry Railway, Rhymney engines and trains worked through on excursions to Barry Island. The usual service eventually became 16 trains on weekdays with three on Sundays on the Rhymney line; the Senghenydd branch service consisted of 12 trains on weekdays only. The joint lines to Merthyr and Dowlais had eight trains a day provided by the Rhymney, GWR passenger workings being minimal.

Goods services started with 12 open wagons, 20 vans and two cattle wagons. Only a minimum of extra stock was ordered during the early years of financial restraint. However after the early 1870s additional wagons were quickly obtained to relieve the previously embarrassing shortages. To the end of its days the Rhymney Railway obtained most of its additional wagon stock from outside manufacturers but most of the replacement wagons were built by themselves, first in the Cardiff and afterwards in the Caerphilly shops. C. T. Hurry Riches standardised on the 1903 RCH wagon with 18ft 0in over headstocks and a 9ft 9in wheel base; goods brake vans, open wagons and vans were all eventually built to this standard. Among the more interesting renewals was the use of old engine and tender frames to build roll and bolster wagons. These were entered in the Rhymney Railway Wagon Register as newly built stock and the last of these interesting renewals was withdrawn by British Railways in 1960 aged 101 years; At the grouping the Rhymney handed over 1,200 goods and departmental wagons.

Above right: To make up for wartime depreciations the Rhymney Railway ordered a batch of bogie coaches from the Gloucester Carriage & Wagon Co. Here is a maker's photograph of Third No 56; as GWR No 1090 it was fitted to work as an intermediate auto-trailer in 1950 and worked as such until withdrawal in 1958. *WRRC*

Right: Though the Gloucester bogie coaches were of an up to date design for their time, their interiors were a bit spartan with wooden slatted seats. One presumes that they were intended for workmen's coaches, leaving the upholstered six-wheeled coaches for other passengers. *WRRC*

106

Up to 1910 the Rhymney used a flat-bottomed rail for its permanent way, but from that year on it fell into line with the majority and used bullhead rails for all subsequent relayings. Like its neighbours, the signals adopted were of the McKenzie & Holland somersault pattern.

As its financial position improved, many station buildings were renewed in dressed stone, usually with the booking office on an over bridge spanning the platforms.

The Rhymney Railway became a constituent company of the GWR group on 25 March 1922, having passed from a penniless concern to a prosperous railway and become one of the best investments of its day — its lucky shareholders regularly received dividends of 9% on its ordinary shares in its later years. Nor was the railway neglected by grouping, the wartime arrears of maintainance had been caught up with, every thing was in first class order, of sound design and built with a view to further expansion.

Top: An up Cardiff-Rhymney train headed by a 2-4-2ST arrives at Bargoed Junction, one of the original stations of 1858, a stone-built structure with the booking office on a bridge spanning the tracks. Several other Rhymney stations were built to this pattern. The up platform was an island, the outer face served the trains of the B&MR. *Courtesy S. Croall*

Above: The original passenger terminus at Adams Street was relegated to goods only when a new station was brought into use on 1 April 1871; this was successively called Crockherbtown, Parade and Cardiff (Rhymney). It was a small clap-boarded building, the road frontage of which is seen here in 1920. The Parade station was closed in 1928 when a new junction between the TVR and Rhymney sections was brought into use and passenger sevices were diverted into the enlarged Queen Street station of the former TVR. *Courtesy B. Stevens*

Above right: The Parade station was laid out with staggered platforms, and this photograph shows the arrival platform in 1920, with the Cardiff Railway railmotorset in its siding beyond the platform. The signals and track in the background are of the TVR. *Courtesy B. Stevens*

Right: Dowlais (Cae Harris), the terminus of the RR-GWR joint Taff-Bargoed line, opened in 1876. Here it is seen with a Dowlais Iron Co train in the middle siding. The far sidings on the left gave a direct connection with the Iron Works, one of whose chimneys can be seen directly behind the coaches. *Courtesy B. Stevens*

The South Wales Mineral Railway

This railway was incorporated by an Act of Parliament on 15 August 1853 as a broad gauge railway. It was to build a mineral railway from exchange sidings at Briton Ferry to North Rhondda Collieries. The route was up the cable-worked Ynys y Maerdy Incline (which was 1½ miles in length and over which locomotives as well as wagons were to pass up and down), through the hills to Tonmawr from whence into the Pelena Valley, through the Gyfychi Tunnel to gain the Afan Valley and then up to Glyn Corrwg at Cymmer, from where it connected to collieries along the Corrwg, eventually terminating at the North Rhondda Colliery.

The first sod was cut on 4 January 1856, from which date the SWMR was leased to the Glyncorrwg Company. Progress was slow because of difficulties in raising the capital, coupled with the failure of the original contractor.

The first section of the west end of the Gyfylchi Tunnel was opened on 1 September 1861; the rest of the railway up to Glyncorrwg was completed on 10 March 1863.

The Glyncorrwg Co became a limited company on 17 February 1859, and 10 years later it became the Glyncorrwg Colliery Co Ltd. It gave as its main objectives: purchasing or leasing and working of mines in or near Glyncorrwg; holding shares in and advancing moneys to the SWMR; and the leasing and working of that railway.

In 1872, when the GWR abandoned the broad gauge in Wales, the SWMR had no choice but to follow suit, selling all its broad gauge locomotives to the GWR except for one that was regauged to standard gauge.

For 40 years the SWMR struggled against the limitations placed upon it by the Ynys y Maerdy

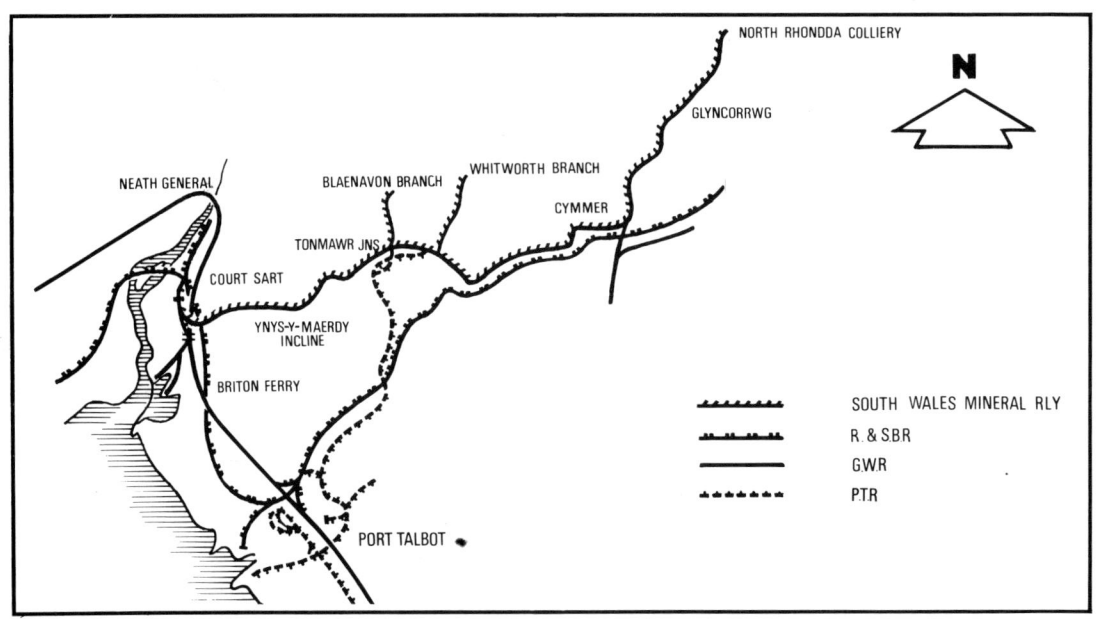

108

Below: One of the four Wolverhampton-built '645' 0-6-0STs as sold to the SWMR. This photograph, taken about 1900, shows one of these engines in original condition except for the addition of a 'Peckett' type cab which enclosed the coal bunker as well. Two of the engines were retained by the Glyncorrwg Colliery Co in 1908, but the two the GWR acquired were condemned in 1910. *Courtesy A. Rees*

incline as the tonnage of coal shipped gradually increased.

The Port Talbot Railway opened its mineral railway from Tonygroes Junction to Tonmawr Junction on 14 November 1898. From this date it took over the SWMR's Blaenavon and Whitworth branches and diverted the traffic to its own dock at Port Talbot.

Very soon there were moves for the PTR to take over the rest of the SWMR, though in 1907 the SWMR obtained an act to construct a deviation railway to replace the Ynys y Maerdy incline. As the company made no attempt to implement this railway, one must suspect that it was a counter move to obtain the best terms possible from the PTR under the agreement which was eventually signed between them on 14 December 1907. As the PTR had itself entered into an agreement by which its railway was to be worked by the GWR, this in reality meant that the SWMR was worked by the GWR from 30 March 1908. Subsequently the Ynys y Maerdy incline was completely closed from June 1910.

The early history of the rolling stock of the SWMR is obscure because between 1877 and 1888 no returns were made and those that were made are suspect. The difficulty of accurate records probably lay in the problem of who actually owned various items of rolling stock — the railway or the colliery company.

Manning Wardle of Leeds supplied three broad gauge engines between 1863 and 1866; only one of these was converted to standard gauge in 1872. Named *Princess* this engine survived till 1901. All the other broad gauge engines were sold at this time — these are believed to have numbered three, but the SWMR was only returning a total of three engines at the time.

The GWR supplied the SWMR with three of its '645' 0-6-0STs — as they were not given GWR works numbers, it appears that they were

built specially for the SWMR. A further engine of this class, GWR No 767, was purchased by the Glyncorrwg Colliery Co in 1875. The four were numbered 1 to 4, and a Black Hawthorn 0-6-0ST became No 5. A further engine was obtained the next year. This is reputed to have been a Manning Wardle. The annual returns give an increase from five to six locomotives in 1891 but the number was reduced again to five in 1898. The last locomotive could have been the *Penylan* that the PTR acquired in 1897. In 1905 two ex-South Devon Railway 0-6-0STs were purchased from the GWR and numbered 6 and 7 by the SWMR.

In 1908 the working agreement with the PTR was superseded by an agreement with the GWR dated 8 October 1908. By this agreement the Glyncorrwg Colliery Co retained two of the Wolverhampton 0-6-0STs, numbered 2 and 4; the remaining locos — Nos 1 and 3 and Nos 5, 6 and 7 — were handed over to the GWR, who withdrew Nos 1, 3 and 5 during 1910-11. The replacements were three Wolverhampton 0-6-0STs of the '1501' class, a development of the '645' class.

The main shed on the SWMR was at Briton Ferry though there was a small outpost at Glyncorrwg from the early days; this survived as a stabling point till 1965.

A passenger service was never officially run by the SWMR, though there is evidence that at holiday times and Neath Fair days that colliery wagons were swept out and trips were run for employees and their families between Glyncorrwg and Briton Ferry. Thankfully there were never any incidents whilst they were passing over the Ynys y Maerdy incline or casualties would have been heavy and drawn the attention of the Railway Inspectorate to these peculiar services. The SWMR had a collection of second-hand coaches for its colliers' trains — Six four-wheeled coaches were returned in 1905 though it is certain

that they were obtained before this. In 1908 it handed over six ex-Great Eastern Railway coaches plus five others of unknown parentage. The GWR withdrew most of them straight away, replacing them with four-wheeled stock of its own.

A passenger service was run between Cymmer and Glyncorrwg between March 1918 and 22 September 1930. Four trains each way were run with extras on Saturdays. The collier's trains survived until 1958, after which date they only ran between Glyncorrwg and the North Rhondda Halt. In 1963 the service was further cut back to the South Pit Halt and finally withdrawn from 30 October 1964.

The first goods wagon the SWMR returned was a solitary goods brake van in 1871. By 1889 the number had increased to two brake vans and five other wagons. In 1908 the GWR took over three goods brakes, three vans and seven ballast wagons. There are no records of makers or even dimensions and most of them were condemned on the spot by the GWR. The SWMR was latterly worked by means of the electric train staff between Glyncorrwg and Tonmawr Junction with an intermediate instrument at Cymmer so that trains could terminate and start from the sidings there.

Under the grouping act the SWMR was absorbed by the GWR on 19 January 1923.

The Taff Vale Railway

The mighty Taff Vale Railway with its proud motto *Cymru a fu, a Chymru a Fydd* ('Wales is, and Wales shall be') was incorporated by Act of Parliament dated 21 June 1836. It was promoted by a group of South Wales industrialists to build a railway from Cardiff to Merthyr Tydfil with a line from Cardiff to Cogan Pill where a trans-shipping dock was to be constructed. The act was granted despite the opposition of the Glamorgan Canal Company, which — along with the historic Penydarren Tramroad and other plate ways — had been built to relieve pressure on the canal between Quaker's Yard and Abercynon. Despite this the canal had reached saturation point in the 1830s with a total capacity of 100,000 tons of coal and iron.

The first engineer of the TVR was I. K. Brunel, who laid it out as a standard gauge railway with no other purpose but to carry heavy industrial products down to the coast for shipping — this was to be a great source of embarrassment to him afterwards. The line to Cogan Pill was abandoned and what proved to be a very restrictive agreement with the Bute Estates was entered into for dock facilities at Cardiff which the Bute Estates were in the process of constructing.

The first section of the TVR to be opened was the single line from Cardiff to Abercynon on 9 October 1840; the rest of the railway to Merthyr was opened on 12 April 1841. The branch line up the Rhondda to collieries at Dinas was opened in June of the same year.

The early years were very difficult with very little return for the capital expended. This made the directors reluctant to build all the branch lines authorised or embark upon fresh extensions. The Dowlais branch, by its amended act which allowed the Dowlais Iron Company to build their own railway including an incline 350ft in height, was brought into use on 21 August 1851. A subsidiary company, the Aberdare Railway, obtained its act on 31 July 1845, and was opened the following year from Abercynon to Gadlys Junction where connections were made with the then broad gauge Vale of Neath Railway.

By 1850 the TVR began to justify the foresight of its promotors when a dividend of 6% was paid; however, this was but a foretaste of the lucrative years ahead.

The Rhondda branch was completed to Treherbert on 7 August, 1856, while the mineral branch up the Rhondda Fach from Porth crept up to Ferndale in 1876 and reached Maerdy. Passenger trains commenced running to Treherbert on 7 August 1863, the branch passenger trains were extended to Maerdy in 1889.

The Ynysybwl branch opened for mineral traffic in 1886, while the Llancaiach branch was opened in stages from Pontypridd between 1844 and 1887 to a junction with the Vale of Neath line.

The rapid development of the coal shipment traffic soon overwhelmed the TVR's leased facilities at the Bute West Dock. In an attempt to ease the congestion a nominally independent company — the Penarth Harbour, Dock & Railway — was incorporated by acts of 1856 and 1857. Opened to Penarth in August 1859, the first dock was brought into use in 1865. The TVR leased the PHDR in 1862 despite the opposition of the Bute Estates, who nevertheless managed to have a restrictive clause preventing the TVR from charging less in dock dues at Penarth than the Bute Estates were charging at Cardiff. The TVR extended Penarth Docks in 1884. A further ease-ment was obtained in 1866 when the TVR was allowed access to the west side of the Bute East Dock in return for not opposing the Rhymney Railway's proposed Caerphilly & Cardiff Railway.

To the west of the main line, the broad gauge South Wales Railway had gained a toe hold in the

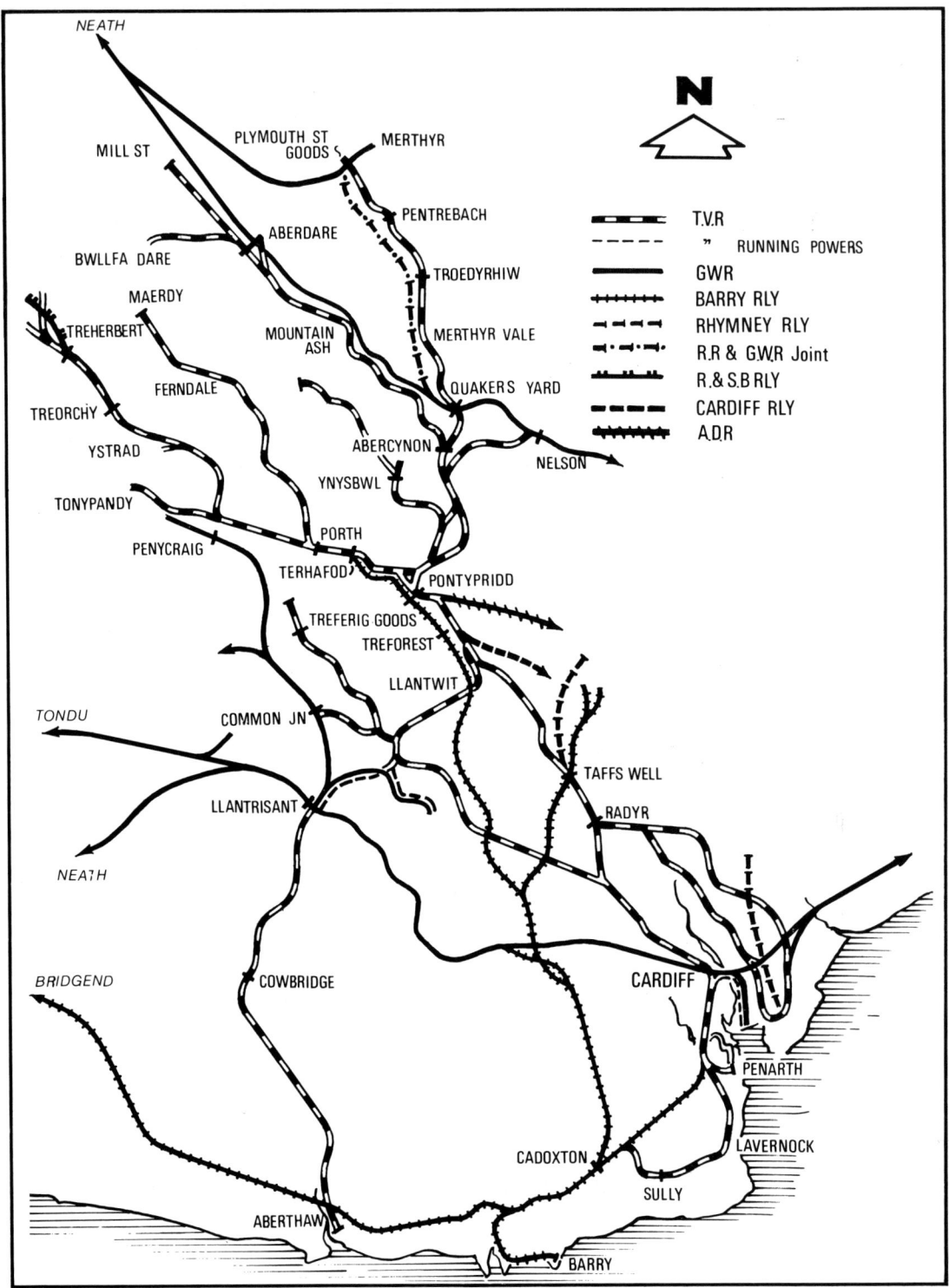

NEATH

MILL ST   PLYMOUTH ST
           GOODS   MERTHYR

           ABERDARE   PENTREBACH

BWLLFA DARE   TROEDYRHIW

MAERDY
TREHERBERT   MOUNTAIN   MERTHYR VALE
                  ASH
TREORCHY   FERNDALE   QUAKERS YARD
YSTRAD   ABERCYNON
                  YNYSBWL   NELSON
TONYPANDY
PENYCRAIG   PORTH
           TERHAFOD   PONTYPRIDD

           TREFERIG GOODS
           TREFOREST

           LLANTWIT

TONDU
           COMMON JN
                                   TAFFS WELL
           LLANTRISANT   RADYR

NEATH

BRIDGEND   COWBRIDGE   CARDIFF

                                   PENARTH

                                   LAVERNOCK
                 CADOXTON
                      SULLY
     ABERTHAW
                      BARRY

T.V.R
      " RUNNING POWERS
      GWR
      BARRY RLY
      RHYMNEY RLY
      R.R & G.W.R Joint
      R.& S.B RLY
      CARDIFF RLY
      A.D.R

N

Rhondda via the Ely Valley Railway, which left the main line of the SWR at Llantrisant and was opened to Penycraig in 1862. The TVR's counter move to this threat was to promote the Llantrisant and Taff Vale Junction Railway which was incorporated on 17 June 1861 to build a railway from Treforest to Maesaraul Junction on the Ely Valley Railway and lay a third rail on that railway to gain access to Llantrisant; A mineral railway from Common Branch Junction to Waterhall Junction on the PHDR opened in 1886. There was also the Treferig Valley Railway opened in 1883 from Common Branch Junction enabling the TVR to tap the Ely Valley traffic.

To the south of Llantrisant the insolvent Cowbridge Railway opened in 1865, was leased by the TVR in 1875 after the latter had worked it for most of its life. Several proposals to extend the Cowbridge Railway along the coast to connect with other railways came to nothing. Finally on 1 October 1892 the Cowbridge & Aberthaw Railway was opened to the lime kilns at Aberthaw, adjacent to the small harbour that was soon to decline.

By 1880, with 8,000,000 tons of coal being shipped through the Bute Docks, the congestion was terrible. Belatedly the Bute Estates began the Roath Dock extensions and its levy of an additional penny per ton on all coal shipped to help finance the constructional costs was the spark that finally ignited the smouldering resentment of the coal owners and shippers. Led by David Davies of the Ocean Coal Co they were determined to smash the Bute monopoly as the slow turn round of wagons was compelling them to introduce short time working while at the same time they were unable to meet their contracts. This made the TVR's coal trains very expensive

to operate, but the company was too complacent at a time when it should have developed alternative shipping facilities themselves. While the Bute Estates and the TVR defeated the Barry Railway Bill in the House of Lords in 1883, presented again the following year with a few amendments, the Barry Railway Bill was passed on 14 August 1884. A TVR counter-proposal — the Cardiff Penarth & Barry Railway — was only allowed to an end on junction with the Barry Railway at Cadoxton and was restricted to local traffic only.

In 1888 the TVR opened its Roath branch, which left the main line at Llandaff and gave the TVR direct access to the new Roath Dock. In later years this was further extended to the Queen Alexandra Dock. But when the Barry Railway opened on 18 July 1889, the immediate effect was a disastrous drop in the revenue of the TVR. The

Below left: The only class of tender engine still in existence at the grouping was the 'K' class and the rebuilds classified 'L'. The TVR was already withdrawing them and all were on the duplicate list. The GWR did very little with them, many being withdrawn without being renumbered. However here is TVR No 325 as GWR No 948 still plodding along at Cathys in 1924. The engine survived to the following June, and the whole class had gone by 1930. *WRRC*

Below: For branch passenger workings T. Hurry Riches brought out three outside-cylinder 4-4-0Ts; Nos 67, 68, 69 — classified 'I' — normally worked the Cowbridge Branch until displaced by the introduction of railmotor cars. Renumbered in the Duplicate List as Nos 285, 286 and 287 they took on a new lease of life when they were equipped for auto-train working with two trailer cars. Here is No 287 on a Cadoxton-Penarth-Cardiff train at Cardiff (Riverside) in 1913. The TVR system of control was by means of unsightly wires in pulley guides coupled over the roofs of the trailers to a ship-type wheel to which they connected to on either side. *WRRC*

ordinary share dividend which had reached $17\frac{1}{2}\%$ in 1882 dropped to 3% in 1890. Recovery from this catastrophe took several years but recover the TVR did, mainly because of the ever increasing demand for Welsh steam coal. The TVR also expanded its passenger services very successfully to augment its receipts. Previously this side of the business had been ignored as impracticable because of the congestion.

The final assault on the TVR came from the chief source of contention, the Bute Dock Co which succeeeded in 1897 in obtaining powers for its own railway line. This ran from Treforest to Heath Junction on the Rhymney Railway and then by means of running powers gained its own dock lines. At the same time the Dock Co changed its name to the Cardiff Railway. This line was brought into use in 1911 but by an oversight connection was only allowed to the passenger lines of the TVR at Treforest. Afterwards the TVR successfully convinced parliament that, because of geographical limitations at Treforest coupled with the volume of traffic passing at this point, it was impossible to position junctions to

connect the Cardiff Railway with the mineral lines of the TVR. Thus the TVR foiled the Cardiff Railway's attempt to siphon off Rhondda coal traffic with its own line.

An attempt by the TVR to fuse its own railway with those of the Cardiff and Rhymney Railways was defeated principally because of the opposition of the Barry Railway and Newport shipping interests.

So at the end of the first decade of the 20th century, the TVR was threatened by: the R&SBR connecting at Treherbert; the Barry Railway siphoning off the cream of the coal traffic at Trehafod and Treforest; the PC&NR diverting more coal away to Newport Docks. The Vale of Neath line of the GWR tapping the Dare Valley; and the RR-GW Taff Bargoed line running up to Merthyr. All these lines vigorously competing for the very traffic the TVR was promoted to carry.

The first passenger engines of the TVR were a pair of 2-2-2 tender engines named *Taff* and *Rhondda*, supplied by Sharp Roberts & Co in 1840. Within a few years they were rebuilt as 0-4-2s and managed to cope with trains until they

Below left: The last batch of Class 'M1' was not vacuum-braked until rebuilt by the TVR to Class M, being regarded as mineral engines. No 180 is seen here at work; note the double smokebox doors. It was previously thought that these had been dispensed with for this batch of engines. *Courtesy C. Batstone*

Above: In order to cope with the increasing auto-train traffic some of the 'M1s' were fitted for these trains in 1910-12. The increased power enabled them to haul two sets of trailers with the engine in the middle. Here is No 14 at Penarth on a Cadoxton bound auto-train in 1921. The large casting in place of the usual front coupling was the TVR rigid auto-train coupling to ensure that tension was maintained on the control wires. *Courtesy H. T. Hobbs*

Above: In 1888 the TVR introduced the first inside-cylinder 4-4-2T in the country. They took over the main line trains though their reign was to be very short. The Class C engines, as they were designated, were always favourites where any special workings were concerned. On 27 June 1912 No 173 took charge of the TVR Royal Train provided to convey King George V to Treherbert, and is seen here passing Llwynypia. *Courtesy C. Batstone*

Below: Class C No 174 was the standby engine for the Royal Train in 1912. It is seen here decorated by the cleaners and fitters who had prepared her for an unidentified occasion. *Courtesy C. Batstone*

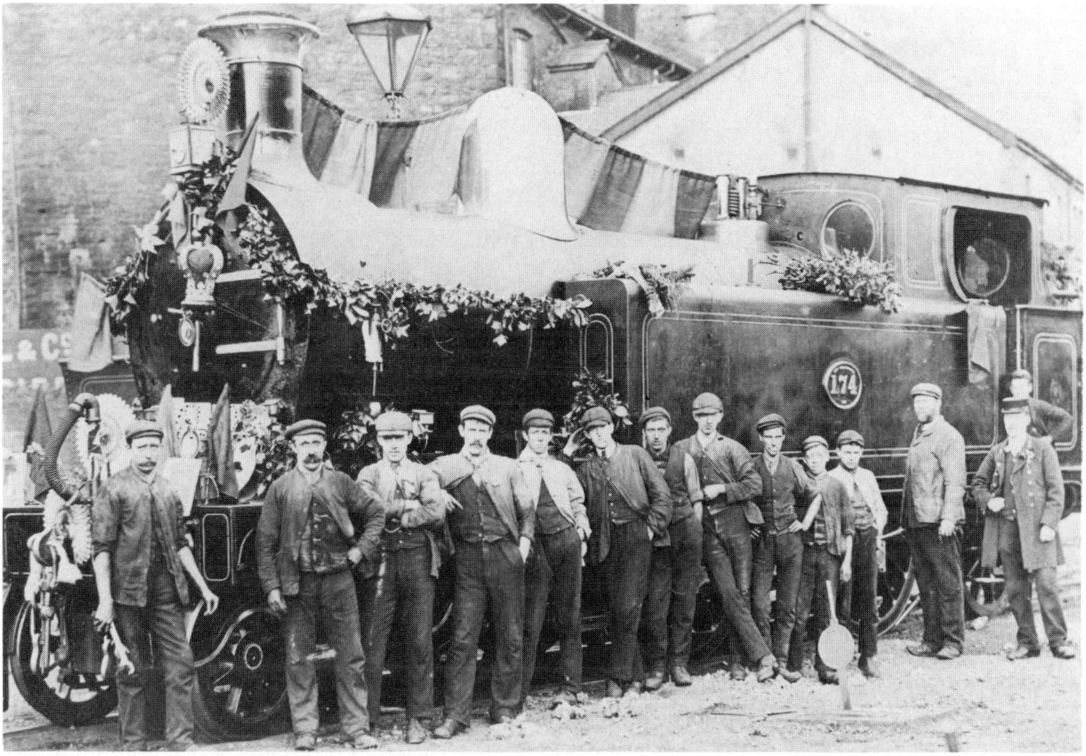

were replaced by a pair of 2-4-0 tender engines supplied by Stothert & Slaughter in 1852. These were assisted by other engines of the same wheel arrangement, the last of which was built in Cardiff in 1878. Also there were 0-4-4Ts rebuilds of old double-framed goods engines; the first of these entered service in 1876, the last in 1883. They managed to cope with the very infrequent service of the times, most of the trains being for colliers and usually worked by mineral engines.

In 1884 T. Hurry Riches turned out from West Yard Works the first outside-cylinder 4-4-0T; another two followed the next year. These three engines — classified 'I' — were the first modern passenger engines of the TVR. Soon displaced from the heavier trains, in later years, they worked from Llantrisant to Cowbridge until displaced by the railmotor cars from 1905. All was not lost, however as the railmotors generated more traffic than they could manage and so the 'I' class re-entered service in December 1907 on auto-trains. Initially they worked between Cardiff, Penarth and Cadoxton with two trailers. Reboilering commenced in 1914, after which they regularly worked with four trailers (two either side of the engine). They did not last long after grouping and the trio was withdrawn at the end of 1925.

Three inside-cylinder 4-4-2Ts arrived in 1888, the first of that wheel arrangement in the country. With their brass chimney caps, domes and other fittings, they took over the main line trains and were classified 'C'. Three more followed from the Vulcan Foundry in 1891 but unfortunately their reign on the main line passenger trains was very short. The drive to develop this service after the opening of the Barry Railway was so successful that they could no longer cope with the increased weight of those trains. Transferred to the heavier branch line trains they remained the automatic choice for any special duties as when on 27 June 1912 No 173 hauled the Royal Train to Treherbert. During 1917 they were fitted for auto-train working and were usually to be found sandwiched in the middle of four trailers. But they did not last long under the GWR, and all were withdrawn by 1927.

T. Hurry Riches' answer to the increasing weight of passenger trains was a passenger version of his highly successful 0-6-2T. With 5ft 3in coupled wheels, eight engines were built by

Right, top to bottom: In 1899 a further nine engines classified as '02' arrived. There were detail differences between them and their predecessors. After grouping the GWR did little with them, all were withdrawn by the end of 1928 being displaced by the '56XX' class engines. One of them, No 85 as GWR No 426, was sold to the Lanton, Hetton & Joicey Collieries and gave service till the early 1960s. Here is No 44 on Cathays shed in 1920. *WRRC*

The last class to be introduced by T. Hurry Riches — 1908-10 — was the '04' class of 41 engines. A much larger engine than that of previous classes, the '04s' worked main line passenger and coal trains until grouping. All except five were rebuilt with Swindon taper boilers, and were used away from their original haunts. The whole class was intact at nationalisation but scrapping commenced in 1948 and all were gone by 1955. here is No 110, a Beyer Peacock-built engine, trundling down through Taffs Well with yet another train load of coal for shipment. *WRRC*

Class '04' No 119, also built by Beyer Peacock, at Cogan Junction in 1919, working trips to Penarth. *WRRC*

Former TVR No 6 — one of the five engines never rebuilt with a Swindon boiler. Except for the GWR replacement cab and bunker and other detail alterations, No 6's TVR origin is still apparent. It is seen on Cardiff Canton shed on 22 August 1948; nine months later it made the final trip to Swindon. *WRRC*

the Vulcan Foundry in 1895. Classified 'U', they proved to be speedy engines and deserved their nickname of 'highflyers'. A further batch of seven followed the next year; these had a small radial wheel of 3ft 1in diameter and became Class 'U1'. In their shining black livery with gleaming brass beading and excellent steaming qualities, they reigned supreme until gradually displaced by the Cameron 'A' class engines. After grouping two were rebuilt with taper boilers, the remainder altered but little. They were all withdrawn by 1930, the two taper boiler rebuilds following them the next year.

After the death of T. Hurry Riches in 1911, his former assistant J. Cameron succeeded him and designed a mixed traffic 0-6-2T. This design retained the 5ft 3in coupled wheel but had a high pitched Belpaire boiler without smokebox wing plates and other modifications. It was a most powerful looking engine and successive batches appeared between 1914 and 1921 from various makers until a class of 58 engines was formed. They took over most of the passenger duties and did little goods working before the grouping.

Above: GWR No 279, originally TVR No 2, was given the full rebuild at Swindon Works in 1928 after which it returned to service like this. Swindon rebuilding usually included GWR type square cornered water tanks. *WRRC*

Above right: As part of the drive to increase passenger traffic after the opening of the Barry Railway, T. Hurry Riches introduced his highly successful 'U' and 'U1' classes (the only difference was in the radial wheels). They dominated the passenger workings until the arrival of the Cameron Class As. Here in 1920 is the first engine of the class, No 191, reduced to secondary trains. *WRRC*

Below: Trehebert shed cleaners with No 195 as prepared for service on Coronation Day 1902. The engine looks clean enough to work a royal train for King Edward VII. *Courtesy C. Batstone*

While quite speedy engines, drivers tended to restrain them to avoid the rolling that the higher pitched boiler caused. Also there were steaming difficulties that were not entirely cured before grouping. The GWR took the drastic remedy of reboilering the entire class between 1925 and 1932, at the same time they received Swindon pattern coal bunkers and in some cases side tanks as well. They remained on passenger duties until 1953 when they were displaced by the British Railways Class 3 2-6-2Ts. Withdrawal commenced and by 1957 the entire class was no more.

For its mineral trains the TVR commenced its services with four double-framed 0-4-2 tender engines built by Hawthorne & Co in 1841. Additional engines of the same wheel arrange-

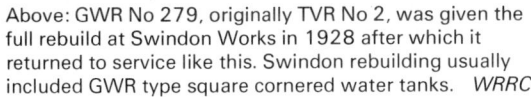

ment followed from other makers as did three second-hand 4-2-0 Yankee engines from the Birmingham & Gloucester Railway in 1845. The more powerful 0-6-0 was soon adopted, the first arriving in 1846 built by Hick & Son of Bolton. In 1859 the first double-framed 0-6-0 was constructed in West Yard Works; ultimately the class consisted of 45 engines, the last one being completed in 1872. With other engines of the same wheel arrangement, the TVR struggled to maintain its expanding coal traffic.

In 1874 the first single-framed 0-6-0 was built by Kitson & Co. Eventually 85 of these were built, at the West Yard Works. They proved to be a very successful design and worked the heaviest mineral trains. For many years they were classified as 'L', but when they were rebuilt with a higher pressed and modified boilers from 1892, they became Class K. In later years when further reboilering and cannibalisation took place, the two classes became indistinguishable. The first withdrawals occurred in 1907, but World War 1 slowed this process down and by grouping there were still 42 in service, though their days were numbered. All were gone by 1927 except for old No 298 which lasted till 1930.

In 1885 T. Hurry Riches introduced the first 0-6-2Ts to be seen on Welsh railways; these were built by Kitson & Co who had just built similar engines for the Lancashire & Yorkshire Railway. Classed as mixed traffic engines, the earlier ones did a considerable amount of passenger duties in their early years. Built in batches up to 1892, they became Class M and soon proved their worth as the ideal engine for South Wales. When they were

gradually displaced from the mineral workings, they increased their passenger workings on the branch lines, and also through workings to other railways where their light axle loading was an advantage. Finally in December 1910 No 163 was fitted for auto-train working, and it soon proved that a six-coupled engine was a decided advantage for rapid acceleration from frequent halts. Further engines were fitted by the TVR and after the grouping the GWR fitted some of them with its own form of auto-train gear. Scrapping commenced in 1925 and the last survivors were the GWR auto-trains which were withdrawn in 1934. One sold to the Longmoor Military Railway lasted till 1944.

In 1891 10 engines arrived from Kitson's. These were fitted with an enlarged boiler similar to those fitted to the 'C' class 4-4-2Ts, but otherwise practically identical to the 'M' class. Also classed as mixed traffic engines, they became Class N and did not do much passenger work, mainly being employed on the coal trains. No 187 was fitted for auto-train working in 1913, but the GWR did little with them and most were still in TVR condition when withdrawn. No 107 was the last survivor and was withdrawn in 1934.

During 1894-5 West Yard Works built six engines that became Class O, with a boiler pressure of 150lb and coupled wheels $\frac{1}{2}$in larger than the 'M' and 'N' classes. Vacuum-fitted from new, they were again classed as mixed traffic engines. After an initial period on the coal trains, they became shunting and yard pilots and were withdrawn by 1930 after little alteration by the GWR; two were sold to colliery companies.

Bottom far left: Penarth Dock station in 1920 with 'U1' No 196 on a Cadoxton train. Too heavy for most of the branches the 'U1s' were working coal trains at this time. *C. W. Clifford courtesy C. C. Green*

Bottom left: In 1914 John Cameron introduced the first of his 'A' class mixed traffic engines, which did little until grouping but haul main line passenger trains. The last members of the class were delivered in 1921 when they totalled 58. A powerful looking engine, they introduced new features to the TVR. The 'A' class was not as popular with the enginemen who worked them, the higher pitched boiler made them pitch and roll more than their predecessors; there were also steaming difficulties. If the TVR had retained its independence longer, doubtless the problem would have been rectified without much expenditure, but the GWR rebuilt the whole class with taper boilers and other Swindon features. Here is No 165 working from Merthyr in the summer of 1920 as delivered by Hawthorn Leslie in plain black livery. *WRRC*

Right, top to bottom: No 416 seen soon after delivery from the Vulcan Foundry in 1921 calling at Cardiff GWR in plain black livery with the addition of a crest on the bunker. No 416 was the highest TVR engine number. *Courtesy H. T. Hobbs*

Former TVR No 157 was rebuilt at Caerphilly in 1929, but whatever the rebuild might have done, it did little for No 157's looks. The Swindon taper boiler never seemed to fit the rebuilt 'As'. As GWR No 379, this engine was withdrawn in 1956. *WRRC*

Halted at signals in Cardiff General station whilst working a goods trip is GWR No 381. The former TVR No 159 survived to the very end and was withdrawn in August 1957, when with one swoop the last seven survivors went in one month. *WRRC*

T. Hurry Riches developed the steam railcars to combat competition from tramways being electrified at the time, and as a more economic means of providing a service over branch lines with limited traffic. Here is railmotor No 9 very soon after entering service in 1905; the location is believed to be on the Ynsybwl branch. As originally built, the railmotors had no front coupling or brake pipe connection at the front end; this was soon altered so that extra vehicles could be attached. *Courtesy R. Wilding*

Above: To serve the Pwllyrhebog branch with its cable-worked incline of 1 in 13 easing to 1 in 29, T. Hurry Riches designed three locomotives. They had 5ft 3in wheels to give clearance for the cable as they propelled their train up the incline attached to the cable. The coned boiler was to ensure that the firebox crown was adequately covered with water at the same time. Here is the first engine — No 141 — at Tonypandy in 1905; the locomotives remained here until the incline closed in 1951 when No 141 — by then GWR No 193 — was sold to the NCB and worked at Caerphilly until 1960. *Courtesy C. Batstone*

Right: The Aerw branch was a single line for access to the Cymmer Collieries of Insoles Ltd. This photograph of 1915 shows the second TVR signalbox to see service; one or two boxes of this pattern survive to this day. *Courtesy C. Batstone*

Below: This signalbox which controlled the junctions between the Treherbert line and the Maerdy branch was at Rhondda Fach Junction at Porth. Erected in the 'V' of the junction on a very restricted site, it was an unusual structure wider at one end than the other; this was accentuated by an extension that doubled its length, as illustrated in 1910. *Courtesy C. Batstone*

Top left: At the same time the photographer took this interior view of the Rhondda Fach Junction box. The TVR's practice in its larger signalboxes can be seen: the signalman with his Block bells and instruments is behind the desk on the left; the gentlemen on the frame are pointsmen under his direction. Gas lighting is provided by old fish tailed gas jets that were made obsolete by the introduction of mantles. *Courtesy C. Batstone*

Left: An important part of railway services was the humble horse dray collecting and delivering parcels and goods as this one is doing round the streets of Pontypridd in 1910. *Courtesy C. Batstone*

Below: The original station of Pontypridd in 1880 with staff and shunting horse in the main line platforms with the Rhondda bay on the right. Inadequate for the increasing traffic it was rebuilt between 1906 and 1911 without ceasing operations. *Courtesy C. W. Harris*

Above: Aberaman station in 1900; this the last station on the Dare branch before Aberdare was opened by the Aberdare Railway in 1846.
Courtesy Cynon Valley Libraries

Right: Aberdare in 1919 with a 'K' class 0-6-0 and 'O' class 0-6-2T with two mineral brakevans to work coal trains. The white patches behind the hand rails were a 1914-18 wartime expedient.
Courtesy Cynon Valley Libraries

Six more engines arrived from Kitson's in 1894 and six more were built in the West Yard Works in 1897. These were the last engines the TVR built for themselves; they were classified 'O1' and were very similar to the preceding class. After the grouping the GWR rebuilt two with their taper boilers but all were withdrawn by 1931. Two were sold for further service; one — No 28 — was sold to the Longmoor Military Railway where it was named *Gordon*. *Gordon* was sold again in 1947 to the South Hetton Colliery Co and was finally withdrawn in 1960 when it was presented by the NCB to the British Transport Commission for preservation. After some years of uncertainty it was eventually acquired by the National Museum of Wales and is currently being restored by the Caerphilly Railway Society.

The next development was the arrival of the nine engines of Class O2 from Nielson, Reid & Co in 1899. These were basically 'O1s' with the refinements introduced by the 'U' and 'U1' classes. After grouping they acquired GWR safety valve bonnets but little else. TVR No 31 had the unhappy distinction of being the last engine to have a repair in West Yard Works in 1926. All were withdrawn by 1928. TVR No 85 was sold for colliery service and, after withdrawal in 1968, was acquired by the Keighley & Worth Valley Railway for preservation.

Fifteen engines built in three batches between 1902 and 1905 were classified as 'O3s'; with larger fireboxes they were mainly used as passenger engines until displaced by the Cameron 'A' class. Rebuilt after the grouping with various

Left: Ystrad station with the arrival of the 5pm train on 12 April 1912; it is composed of a set of six-wheeled coaches. *Courtesy C. Batstone*

Below left: Ystrad sidings in 1880 an 'L' class ready to work a train of the celebrated Ocean steam coal. This would be from the Maindy Colliery — the first one sunk by David Davies in 1865-66, at an initial outlay of £38,000. After this he never looked back. *Courtesy M. E. Morton Lloyd*

Below: A train of coal wagons drifts into Tylorstown in 1920. This section of the Rhondda Fach branch was opened in 1856. Tylorstown station site was very cramped, the little mileage yard behind the signalbox being gated off from the rest of the railway. *Courtesy B. Stevens*

spare TVR boilers, some additionally received GWR cabs, tanks and coal bunkers. All were withdrawn by 1934 except for two rebuilt engines (TVR Nos 18 and 19) which served through World War 2 and were still around to be nationalised before withdrawal in 1948.

The final Hurry Riches' development was the 'O4' class which consisted of 41 engines built in four batches between 1907 and 1910. These had little in common with previous classes — the wheelbase was increased by 13in and a longer boiler with an enlarged firebox was fitted, and a longer cab — and they did not present such a well-proportioned appearance as previous engines. Initially the 'O4s' worked main line coal and passenger trains. After the grouping the GWR intended to rebuild the entire class with taper boilers, but four of them — TVR Nos 6, 17, 48 and 104 — retained their TVR boilers to the end. Withdrawals began in 1948 and went ahead at a rapid rate. The last four were withdrawn in 1955.

While the TVR's development of additional passenger revenue was very successful, there was a need to find a way to work some of the lighter branches economically. At the same time other services were losing traffic to the recently introduced electric tramways. After considering petrol and electric railcars, T. Hurry Riches built his first steam railcar in the West Yard Works in 1903. Somewhat surprisingly, the two axles of the engine unit were uncoupled, after the elimination of initial problems with over heated bearings with Railmotor No 1 in 1904. Six more practically

Above: The officers and men of the Somerset Light Infantry after detraining at Tonypandy in 1911. They were brought in to maintain law and order following the upsurge of unrest occasioned by the severity of the Cambrian coal strike; they were commanded by Sir Neville MacReady, who in 1920-22 was in charge of the 'Black and Tans' in Ireland.
Courtesy C. Batstone

Right: Considering its heavy gradients and the sheer volume of traffic it moved over its lines, the TVR had only three fatal accidents involving passengers. The last was the rear end collision at Coke Ovens on 23 January 1911 when 11 passengers were killed. The strong band of police were already available because of the Cambrian Colliery strike.
Courtesy C. Batstone

Above: To those who believe the Rhondda is a scene of industrial desolation, here is the setting of the Pentre Colliery of Cory Bros with a train of their empty wagons awaiting entry to the reception sidings.
Courtesy C. Batstone

identical railmotors were obtained from the Avonside Engine Co in 1904. A further six were obtained from Kerr Stuart & Co in 1905 with third class accommodation only. Finally, in 1906, four enlarged engine units were obtained from Manning Wardle — the coach work consisted of three bodies and was supplied by the Brush Electrical Co. These units were an attempt to provide additional power to work an extra trailer on some of the more steeply graded branches. Even these were not entirely successful and the first auto-train sets were adapted. By this time T. Hurry Riches had become a railmotor devotee and had presented several papers on them to various professional bodies. So the TVR engine men had no alternative but to persevere with them until John Cameron withdrew them as they wore themselves out, adapting some of the coach bodies as trailers for auto-trains. All the engine units were disused or scrapped by grouping.

The original coaches of the TVR were the typical small four-wheeled stock of the times. Additions and replacements were soon being built at the West Yard Works where the last four-wheelers were constructed in 1891. They were invariably replaced by bogie coaches and six-wheeled brake vans.

The usual main line train for Merthyr and Treherbert consisted of four bogie coaches with a six-wheeled brake van at either end plus an additional two bogie coaches and a further six-wheeled brake van for the Maerdy and Aberdare branches respectively. On the latter the additional coaches were detached and attached at Porth and Abercynon. The remainder of the branches and workmen's services were usually worked by sets of four-wheeled coaches. At least two 10-coach sets on the Penarth branch contained a four-wheeled first saloon with a clerestory roof.

This was used exclusively as a club car by Cardiff coal and shipping magnates on their daily journey from Penarth — the top residential district of the day. As part of its programme of speeding up train services, the TVR employed assistant guards who rode in the front brake vans of trains and took charge of most of the parcels traffic for intermediate stations, the head guard

Right: Former TVR 'M' class No 168, renumbered 579 by the GWR and sold to the Longmoor Military Railway in 1927 where it was named *Kitchener*. Seen on the LMR in 1930; the only visible alteration is its GWR safety valve bonnet; afterwards named *Wellington* it was finally scrapped towards the end of the last war. *WRRC*

riding in the rear van. Often the same pair of men worked together for years, but after the grouping the GWR soon dispensed with the services of the assistant guards. Also it was usual to turn engines at the end of every trip so that they always worked chimney first, but again grouping soon saw the end of this practice.

The TVR did not often buy second-hand coaches, but in 1906 and 1907 as it was short of four-wheeled stock for its workmen's trains, it purchased 67 coaches from the Metropolitan District Railway and the Metropolitan District and London Tilbury & Southend Joint Stock Co. The final TVR stock was supplied by Cravens Ltd in 1921; it was of a high eliptical roof design, 60ft in length, which was formed into two sets with one coach less than those composed of the earlier shorter bogie stock. The last of these coaches were withdrawn in 1959.

The majority of the TVR's goods traffic was coal and heavy minerals loaded into private owner wagons. Nevertheless, at grouping the TVR handed over 2,400 goods wagons most of which were open wagons and vans though there was a good selection of special wagons to cater for unusual loads. In its earlier years the TVR was reluctant to use brake vans on its branch and trip workings, but all trains were worked by a guard with a brakesman to assist him right up to grouping.

The earliest signals used were a rudimentary disc and crossbar pattern. The first signalboxes were of a similar pattern to those supplied to the LSWR. Replacement signals were of the somer-sault pattern as supplied by McKenzie & Holland; from the early 1900s the signal arms had twin chevrons and bars painted on them. The TVR controlled trains by means of Tyers one-wire three-position instruments, electric relays and treadles that automatically placed starting signals to danger after the passage of a train. This safeguard was afterwards dispensed with by the GWR as unnecessary.

Latterly the Permanent Way Department used 45ft rails weighing 95lb to the yard.

Many of the station buildings were built in brick or dressed stone with the door and window reveals and corner courses in a glazed yellow brick reminiscent of a certain type of public building. All waiting rooms were provided with a Bible as a bequest of a deceased director, so that intending passengers could spend their waiting moments quietly preparing themselves for the hereafter.

When the veteran General Manager Ammon Beasley retired in 1917 because of his advancing years, A. E. Prosser of the Rhymney Railway took on the management of the TVR in addition to the Rhymney and Cardiff Railways.

In its final year of independence — 1921 — the TVR carried nearly 8,000,000 tons of coal over its own rails and over 8,000,000 passenger journeys were booked. The ordinary share dividend was 4%, but as the shareholders had received £250 of new shares for every £100 of the original shares this was good.

The TVR joined the GWR group as the second largest constituent company on 25 March 1922